The PICNIC cookbook

MORE THAN 100 RECIPES FOR OUTDOOR FEASTS TO SAVOR AND SHARE WITH FAMILY AND FRIENDS

Mark Greger

ALSO by Mark Greger

a) *The 30-Minute Summer Cookbook: Beat the Heat Everyday With 101 Healthy Recipes for Weight Loss Detox and Cleanse Your Body;*

b) *Energy Smoothie: 101 Keto, Dash and Diabetic Recipes to Supercharge Your Health;*

c) *The 30-Minute Summer Cookbook: Beat the Heat Everyday With 101 Healthy Recipes for Weight Loss Detox and Cleanse Your Body (+30 smoothie recipes);*

d) *Award Winning Bbq Recipes: Everything You Ever Wanted to Know About Barbecue;*

e) *Award winning BBQ sauces: The secret ingredient the next-level smoking;*

f) *The Healthy Smoothies Cookbook: More than100 Tasty Recipes to Lose Weight, feel great, and gain energy in Your Body;*

g) *The Complete Summer Cookbook: 200 Recipes for Weight Loss Detox And Supercharge Your Energy;*

Disclaimer

This publication is designed to provide competent and reliable information regarding the subject matter covered. However, it is sold with the understanding that the author
is not engaged in rendering professional or nutritional advice. Laws and practices often vary from state and country to country and if medical or other expert assistance is required, the services of a professional should be sought. The author specifically disclaims any liability that is
incurred from use or application of the content of this book.

TABLE OF CONTENTS

INTRODUCTION

Spring is the perfect time to use fresh ingredients in your cooking.

Create delicious and portable feasts for any occasion. Call up your friends, grab a blanket, and fill up your picnic basket!

A family picnic adventure is a quick and easy getaway that will surely strengthen your bond and allow everyone to enjoy a happy day. Whether you have it planned or spontaneous, it will always spell a lot of fun.

Sharing food on picnic is the perfect way to entertain family and friends. With minimum effort and maximum impact you can casually host in style, while focusing on spending time together, rather than being stuck in the kitchen. No cooking skills are required to make these boards (and you!) shine!

You will find that even though the recipes are simple, the tastes are quite amazing.

Remember these recipes are unique so be ready to try some new things. Also remember that the style of cooking used in this cookbook is effortless. So even though the recipes will be unique and great tasting, creating them will take minimal effort!

When you go on a picnic, apart from where to go, what to eat is an important consideration. It will now be easier for you to plan your funny meals and spend more meaningful time with the family and your friends.

Food usually spells the difference between a successful day out and a dreary one. If you want everyone to enjoy this day off, this fun getaway, make sure you plan out your menu carefully.

Enjoy!

YUMMY SANDWICH

...such a perfect day for picnicking.

TUNA 'N PECAN SANDWICH

Cooking time: 15 minutes
Serving: 4

Ingredients:
- ❖ 1/3 cup chopped celery
- ❖ 1 small Gala apple, diced
- ❖ 1/3 cup fat-free mayonnaise
- ❖ ¼ cup chopped pecans, toasted
- ❖ ¼ cup green olives, pitted and finely chopped
- ❖ ¼ teaspoon salt ¼ teaspoon freshly ground black pepper
- ❖ 12-ounce tuna in water, drained
- ❖ 4 curly leaf lettuce leaves
- ❖ 4 gluten-free English muffins, split and toasted

Directions:
1. In a medium bowl, flake the tuna with a fork.
2. Stir in the celery, apple, mayonnaise, pecans, olives, salt and pepper in the bowl and combine.
3. Place the English muffins on a plate and place the lettuce leaf on top of each muffin.
4. Then, top the muffin halves with the tuna salad made in step 1.
5. Then cover the salad with the other half of the muffins.
6. Your sandwich is ready to be served!

Nutritional Information:
- ❖ Calories 104
- ❖ Fat 7g
- ❖ Protein 4g
- ❖ Carbohydrates 7g
- ❖ Fiber 0g
- ❖ Cholesterol 21mg
- ❖ Sodium 167mg

BUTTERMILK MAPLE BREAD

Preparation time: 1 h 30 m
Cooking time: 3 h
Serving: 15

Ingredients:
- ❖ 1/2 C. sprouted wheat berries, ground
- ❖ 3/4 C. buttermilk
- ❖ 1 egg 2 tbsp maple syrup
- ❖ 1/2 tsp salt
- ❖ 1/3 tsp baking soda
- ❖ 2 tbsp vital wheat gluten
- ❖ 2 1/4 C. whole wheat flour
- ❖ 1 1/2 tsp active dry yeast

Directions:
1. Rinse 1/2 C. of the raw wheat berries in cool water and drain.
2. In a large bowl of the water, add the berries and soak, covered for 12 hours or overnight.
3. In a colander, drain the berries and keep, covered in a dark place.
4. Rinse for about 3 times a day and they will soon begin to sprout.
5. In a couple of day the sprouts will reach their optimum length of about l/4-inch.
6. Drain the sprouts and in a food processor, grind them.
7. In the bread machine pan, place all the ingredients in the order recommended by the manufacturer.
8. Select the Whole Wheat cycle and Medium Crust setting and press Start.

Nutritional Information
- ❖ Calories 104 kcal
- ❖ Fat 0.9 g
- ❖ Carbohydrates 20.6g
- ❖ Protein 4.9 g
- ❖ Cholesterol 13 mg
- ❖ Sodium 124 mg

* Percent Daily Values are based on a 2,000 calories diet.

BUTTERMILK BROWN SUGAR BREAD ROLLS

Preparation time: 15 m
Cooking time: 20 m
Serving: 12

Ingredients:
- ❖ 3 C. bread flour
- ❖ 1 C. buttermilk
- ❖ 2 tbsp packed brown sugar
- ❖ 1 1/2 tsp kosher salt
- ❖ 1 (.25 oz.) package active dry yeast
- ❖ 1 egg yolk
- ❖ 2 tbsp canola oil stick butter

Directions:
1. In the bread machine pan, place the bread flour, buttermilk, brown sugar, salt, yeast and egg yolk.
2. Select the Dough setting and let the machine to mix the ingredients till moist.
3. Pause the cycle and add the oil, then let the machine continue to the end of the Dough cycle.
4. Grease the cups of the muffin pans and keep aside.
5. Punch down the dough and remove it from the machine.
6. Divide the dough into 12 equal portions and shape into round, smooth rolls.
7. Arrange the rolls into the prepared muffin cups.
8. Cover the rolls with a kitchen towel and keep in the warm place for about 25 minutes.
9. Set your oven to 350 degrees F.
10. Cook in the oven for about 20 minutes.
11. Remove from the oven and immediately, rub the tops of the hot rolls with a stick of the butter for a soft crust.
12. Cool the rolls slightly and serve warm.

Nutritional Information
- ❖ Calories 176 kcal
- ❖ Fat 4.4 g
- ❖ Carbohydrates 28.3g
- ❖ Protein 5.2 g
- ❖ Cholesterol 20 mg
- ❖ Sodium 271 mg

ROAST BEEF AND PROVOLONE SANDWICH

Preparation time: 5 m
Cooking time: 10 m
Serving: 4

Ingredients
- ❖ 1 (10.5 oz.) can beef consommé
- ❖ 1 C. water
- ❖ 1 lb thinly sliced deli roast beef
- ❖ 8 slices provolone cheese
- ❖ 4 hoagie rolls, split lengthwise

Directions
1. Set your oven to 350 degrees before doing anything else.
2. Open your rolls and place them in a casserole dish.
3. Now combine water and beef consommé in a pan to make a broth.
4. Cook your beef in this mixture for 5 mins.
5. Then divide the meat between your rolls and top them with cheese.
6. Cook the rolls in the oven for 6 mins.
7. Enjoy the sandwiches dipped in broth.

Nutritional Information
- ❖ Calories 548 kcal
- ❖ Fat 22.6 g
- ❖ Carbohydrates 40.5g
- ❖ Protein 44.6 g
- ❖ Cholesterol 94 mg
- ❖ Sodium 2310 mg

* Percent Daily Values are based on a 2,000 calories diet.

OREGANO MOZZARELLA SANDWICH

Preparation time: 8 m
Cooking time: 7 m
Serving: 6

Ingredients
- ❖ 1/4 C. unsalted butter
- ❖ 1/8 tsp garlic powder (optional)
- ❖ 12 slices white bread
- ❖ 1 tsp dried oregano
- ❖ 1 (8 oz.) package shredded mozzarella cheese
- ❖ 1 (24 oz.) jar vodka marinara sauce

Directions
1. Turn on the broiler before doing anything else.
2. Get a baking dish and lay half of your bread pieces in it.
3. On top of each piece of bread put some mozzarella.
4. Then top the cheese with the remaining pieces of bread.
5. With a butter knife coat each sandwich with some butter.
6. Then season the butter by applying some oregano and garlic powder.
7. Broil the sandwiches for 4 mins then flip it and apply more butter, oregano, and garlic to its opposite side.
8. Continue broiling the sandwich for another 4 mins.
9. Enjoy with the marinara as a dip.

Nutritional Information
- ❖ Calories 394 kcal
- ❖ Fat 18.3 g
- ❖ Carbohydrates 42g
- ❖ Protein 15 g
- ❖ Cholesterol 46 mg
- ❖ Sodium 1032 mg

* Percent Daily Values are based on a 2,000 calories diet.

BANH MI SANDWICH

Preparation time: 10 m
Cooking time: 5 m
Serving: 4

Ingredients
- ❖ 4 boneless pork loin chops, cut
- ❖ 1/4 inch thick 4 (7 inch)
- ❖ French bread baguettes, split lengthwise
- ❖ 4 tsps mayonnaise, or to taste
- ❖ 1 oz. chili sauce with garlic
- ❖ 1/4 C. fresh lime juice
- ❖ 1 small red onion, sliced into rings
- ❖ 1 medium cucumber, peeled and sliced lengthwise
- ❖ 2 tbsps chopped fresh cilantro salt and pepper to taste

Directions
1. Place your pork chops on a broiling pan and cook everything in the oven for 5 minutes, each side, or until the meat is fully done.
2. Put mayonnaise evenly on the French rolls and also put one pork chop on each roll.
3. Layer some chili sauce over the meat and add some lime juice, while topping it with onion, pepper, cucumber, salt and cilantro.
4. Add some more lime juice just before serving.

Nutritional Information
- ❖ Calories 627 kcal
- ❖ Carbohydrates 72.1 g
- ❖ Cholesterol 124 mg
- ❖ Fat 12.1 g
- ❖ Fiber 3.3 g
- ❖ Protein 55.3 g
- ❖ Sodium 1005 mg

- ❖ * Percent Daily Values are based on a 2,000 calorie diet.

CLUB SUPER SANDWICH

Preparation time: 15 m
Cooking time: 20 m
Serving: 6

Ingredients
- ❖ 1 (1 lb) loaf French bread
- ❖ 2 tbsps prepared horseradish
- ❖ 1/2 lb thinly sliced roast beef
- ❖ 2 tbsps prepared mustard
- ❖ 1/2 lb thinly sliced cooked ham
- ❖ 5 slices Swiss cheese
- ❖ 2 tbsps mayonnaise
- ❖ 1/2 lb thinly sliced cooked turkey
- ❖ 5 slices processed American cheese 1 small onion, thinly sliced
- ❖ 1 tomato, thinly sliced
- ❖ 1/4 C. butter, melted (optional)

Directions
1. Set your oven to 400 degrees before doing anything else.
2. Horizontally cut your bread into 5 long layers.
3. Coat one piece of bread with horseradish then layer your roast beef.
4. Now lay another piece of bread and coat this one with mustard evenly.
5. Lay some Swiss and ham over this piece. Place another piece of bread and top it with mayo, turkey, and cheese.
6. Lay another long slice of bread and coat it with mayo, onions, and tomato.
7. Now lay the final piece of bread.
8. Top the upmost layer of bread with the melted butter and lay the sandwich on a cookie sheet.
9. Cover the entire sheet including the sandwich with some foil then cook the sandwich in the oven for 17 mins.
10. Divide the sandwich into servings.
11. Enjoy.

Nutritional Information
- ❖ Calories 710 kcal
- ❖ Fat 37 g
- ❖ Carbohydrates 47.2g
- ❖ Protein 46.8 g
- ❖ Cholesterol 134 mg
- ❖ Sodium 1934 mg

TOASTED CINNAMON SANDWICH

Preparation time 5 m
Cooking time: 5 m
Serving: 1

Ingredients
- ❖ 2 links pork sausage links
- ❖ 1 slice Cheddar cheese
- ❖ 2 frozen waffles, toasted
- ❖ 1/4 Red Delicious apple, sliced very thin
- ❖ 1/2 tsp cinnamon-sugar

Directions
1. Stir fry your sausage for 6 mins until it is fully done.
2. Lay one piece of cheese on a waffle then place your apples on top of the cheese.
3. Top the apples with the cinnamon-sugar and the sausage.
4. Place the apples over the waffles and slice the sandwich in half.
5. Enjoy.

Nutritional Information
- ❖ Calories 469 kcal
- ❖ Fat 26.6 g
- ❖ Carbohydrates 37.3g
- ❖ Protein 20 g
- ❖ Cholesterol 80 mg
- ❖ Sodium 907 mg

* Percent Daily Values are based on a 2,000 calorie diet.

THE BEST EGG SALAD SANDWICH

Preparation time: 10 m
Cooking time: 15 m
Serving: 4

Ingredients
- ❖ 8 eggs
- ❖ 1/2 C. mayonnaise
- ❖ 1 tsp prepared yellow mustard
- ❖ 1/4 C. chopped green onion salt and pepper to taste
- ❖ 1/4 tsp paprika

Directions
1. Get your eggs boiling in water.
2. Once the water is boiling, shut the heat, place a lid on the pot, and let the eggs sit in the water for 15 mins.
3. Drain the liquid, remove the shells, and dice the eggs.
4. Now grab a bowl, combine: green onions, eggs, mustard, and mayo.
5. Stir the mix until it is smooth and even then top everything with the paprika, some pepper, and salt. Stir the mix again then serve the salad on some warmed bread rolls.
6. Enjoy.

Nutritional Information
- ❖ Calories 344 kcal
- ❖ Fat 31.9 g
- ❖ Carbohydrates 2.3g
- ❖ Protein < 13 g
- ❖ Cholesterol 382 mg
- ❖ Sodium 1351 mg

* Percent Daily Values are based on a 2,000 calorie diet.

PESTO PROVOLONE AMERICAN SANDWICH

Preparation time: 5 m
Cooking time: 10 m
Serving: 1

Ingredients
- ❖ 2 slices Italian bread
- ❖ 1 tbsp softened butter, divided
- ❖ 1 tbsp prepared pesto sauce, divided
- ❖ 1 slice provolone cheese
- ❖ 2 slices tomato
- ❖ 1 slice American cheese

Directions
1. Coat a piece of bread with butter and place the bread in a frying pan with the buttered side facing downwards.
2. Top the bread with 1/2 of the pesto sauce, some tomato, 1 piece of provolone, and 1 piece of American.
3. Grab the other piece of bread and coat it with the rest of the pesto and place the pesto side of the bread on top of the cheese.
4. Coat the top of the bread with more butter and cook the sandwich for 6 mins each side.
5. Enjoy.

Nutritional Information
- ❖ Calories 503 kcal
- ❖ Fat 36.5 g
- ❖ Carbohydrates 24.2g
- ❖ Protein 20.4 g
- ❖ Cholesterol 82 mg
- ❖ Sodium 1108 mg

* Percent Daily Values are based on a 2,000 calorie diet.

CATALINA'S CUBAN SANDWICH

Preparation time: 20 m
Cooking time 5 m
Serving: 4

Ingredients
- ❖ 1 C. mayonnaise
- ❖ 5 tbsps Italian dressing
- ❖ 4 hoagie rolls, split lengthwise
- ❖ 4 tbsps prepared mustard
- ❖ 1/2 lb thinly sliced deli turkey meat
- ❖ 1/2 lb thinly sliced cooked ham
- ❖ 1/2 lb thinly sliced Swiss cheese
- ❖ 1 C. dill pickle slices
- ❖ 1/2 C. olive oil

Directions
1. Get a bowl, combine: Italian dressing and mayo. Coat your bread liberally with the mix.
2. Now add a layer of mustard then: cheese, ham, and turkey.
3. Place some pickles across the sandwich and top the bread with olive oil.
4. Fry the sandwiches for 3 mins each side and flatten the sandwich with a spatula as it cooks.
5. Slice the sandwich into 2 pieces then serve.
6. Enjoy.

Nutritional Information
- ❖ Calories 1096 kcal
- ❖ Fat 84.4 g
- ❖ Carbohydrates 144.1g
- ❖ Protein 43.3 g
- ❖ Cholesterol 127 mg
- ❖ Sodium 3110 mg

* Percent Daily Values are based on a 2,000 calorie diet.

VODKA SAUCE SANDWICH

Preparation time: 8 m
Cooking time: 7 m
Serving:6

Ingredients
- ❖ 1/4 C. unsalted butter
- ❖ 1/8 tsp garlic powder
- ❖ 12 slices white bread
- ❖ 1 tsp dried oregano
- ❖ 1 (8 oz.) package shredded mozzarella cheese
- ❖ 1 (24 oz.) jar vodka marinara sauce

Directions
1. Get your oven's broiler hot before doing anything else.
2. Grab a jelly roll pan and layer 6 pieces of bread in it.
3. Top the bread evenly with some mozzarella then place the remaining bread pieces.
4. Get a bowl, combine: garlic powder and butter. Top the sandwiches with 1 tbsp of the butter mix.
5. Then coat everything with some oregano.
6. Broil the sandwiches for 3 mins then turn the sandwiches over and coat the bread with another tbsp of butter and more oregano.
7. Continue broiling for 3 more mins then divide the sandwiches into 2 pieces.
8. Enjoy dipped in the marinara sauce.

Nutritional Information
- ❖ Calories 394 kcal
- ❖ Fat 18.3 g
- ❖ Carbohydrates 42g
- ❖ Protein 15 g
- ❖ Cholesterol 46 mg
- ❖ Sodium 1032 mg

HONEY HAM SANDWICH

Preparation time: 15 m
Cooking time: 15 m
Serving: 6

Ingredients:
- ❖ 1/2 lb cooked ham, cut into chunks
- ❖ 1/4 onion, sliced 3 tbsps low-fat creamy salad dressing
- ❖ 2 tsps honey
- ❖ 1 tsp prepared mustard
- ❖ 1 tsp Worcestershire sauce
- ❖ 1 tsp dry mustard powder
- ❖ 1 dash hot pepper sauce
- ❖ 1/2 tsp paprika
- ❖ 1/8 tsp salt
- ❖ 1/8 tsp ground white pepper

Directions:
1. Mice your onions and ham in a food processor then place everything in a bowl.
2. Stir in: white pepper, salad dressing, salt, honey, paprika, mustard, hot sauce, Worcestershire, and mustard powder.
3. Place the mix in the fridge until it is chilled and serve on toasted bread.
4. Enjoy.

Nutritional Information:
- ❖ Calories 128 kcal
- ❖ Fat 8.7 g
- ❖ Carbohydrates 4.6g
- ❖ Protein 7.4 g
- ❖ Cholesterol 23 mg
- ❖ Sodium 624 mg

EASY SALMON BURGER

Preparation Time: 15 minutes
Cooking Time: 15 minutes
Servings: 6

Ingredients:
- ❖ 16 ounces pink salmon, minced
- ❖ 1 cup prepared mashed potatoes
- ❖ 1 medium onion, chopped
- ❖ 1 stalk celery, finely chopped
- ❖ 1 large egg, lightly beaten
- ❖ 2 tablespoons fresh cilantro, chopped
- ❖ 1 cup breadcrumbs Vegetable oil, for deep frying
- ❖ Salt and freshly ground black pepper

Directions:
1. Combine the salmon, mashed potatoes, onion, celery, egg, and cilantro in a mixing bowl.
2. Season to taste and mix thoroughly.
3. Spoon about 2 tablespoon mixture, roll in breadcrumbs, and then form into small patties.
4. Heat oil in a non-stick frying pan.
5. Cook your salmon patties for 5 minutes on each side or until golden brown and crispy.
6. Serve in burger buns and with coleslaw on the side if desired.

Nutritional Information:
- ❖ Calories 230
- ❖ Fat 7.9 g
- ❖ Carbs 20.9 g
- ❖ Protein 18.9

SALMON SANDWICH WITH AVOCADO AND EGG

Preparation Time: 15 minutes
Cooking Time: 10 minutes
Servings: 4

Ingredients:
- ❖ 8 ounces smoked salmon, thinly sliced
- ❖ 1 medium ripe avocado, thinly sliced
- ❖ 4 large poached eggs
- ❖ 4 slices whole-wheat bread
- ❖ 2 cups arugula or baby rocket
- ❖ Salt and freshly ground black pepper

Directions:
1. Place 1 bread slice on a plate top with arugula, avocado, salmon, and poached egg.
2. Season with salt and pepper.
3. Repeat the procedure for the remaining ingredients.
4. Serve and enjoy.

Nutritional Information:
- ❖ Calories: 310
- ❖ Fat: 18.2 g
- ❖ Carbohydrates: 16.4 g
- ❖ Protein: 21.3 g

SALMON SPINACH AND COTTAGE CHEESE SANDWICH

Preparation Time: 15 minutes
Cooking Time: 10 minutes
Servings: 4

Ingredients:
- ❖ 4 ounces of cottage cheese
- ❖ 1/4 cup chives, chopped
- ❖ 1 teaspoon capers
- ❖ 1/2 teaspoon grated lemon rind
- ❖ 4 smoked salmon 2 cups loose baby spinach
- ❖ 1 medium red onion, sliced thinly
- ❖ 8 slices rye bread Kosher salt and freshly ground black pepper

Directions:
1. Preheat your griddle or Panini press.
2. Mix cottage cheese, chives, capers, and lemon rind in a small bowl.
3. Spread and divide the cheese mixture on 4 bread slices.
4. Top with spinach, onion slices, and smoked salmon.
5. Cover with remaining bread slices.
6. Grill the sandwiches until golden and grill marks form on both sides.
7. Transfer to a serving dish.
8. Serve and enjoy.

Nutritional Information:
- ❖ Calories: 261
- ❖ Fat 9.9 g
- ❖ Carbohydrates 22.9 g
- ❖ Protein 19.9 g

SALMON APPLE SALAD SANDWICH

Preparation Time: 15 minutes
Cooking Time: 10 minutes
Servings: 4

Ingredients:
- ❖ 4 ounces canned pink salmon, drained and flaked
- ❖ 1 medium red apple, cored and diced
- ❖ 1 celery stalk, chopped
- ❖ 1 shallot, finely chopped
- ❖ 1/3 cup light mayonnaise
- ❖ 8 slices whole-grain bread, toasted
- ❖ 8 Romaine lettuce leaves
- ❖ Salt and freshly ground black pepper

Directions:
1. Combine the salmon, apple, celery, shallot, and mayonnaise in a mixing bowl.
2. Season with salt and pepper.
3. Put 1 slice of bread on your plate, top with lettuce and salmon salad, and then covers with another piece of bread—repeat the procedure for the remaining ingredients.
4. Serve and enjoy.

Nutritional Information:
- ❖ Calories: 315
- ❖ Fat 11.3 g
- ❖ Carbohydrates 40.4 g
- ❖ Protein 15.1 g

MAKE ME HAPPY

We'll take a picnic lunch

SALMON FETA AND PESTO WRAP

Preparation Time: 15 minutes
Cooking Time: 10 minutes
Servings: 4

Ingredients:
- ❖ 8 ounces smoked salmon fillet, thinly sliced
- ❖ 1 cup feta cheese
- ❖ 8 Romaine lettuce leaves
- ❖ 4 pita bread
- ❖ 1/4 cup basil pesto sauce

Directions:
1. Place 1 pita bread on a plate.
2. Top with lettuce, salmon, feta cheese, and pesto sauce.
3. Fold or roll to enclose filling.
4. Repeat the procedure for the remaining ingredients.
5. Serve and enjoy.

Nutritional Information:
- ❖ Calories: 379
- ❖ Fat 17.7 g
- ❖ Carbohydrates: 36.6 g
- ❖ Protein: 18.4 g

SALMON CREAM CHEESE AND ONION ON BAGEL

Preparation Time: 15 minutes
Cooking Time: 10 minutes
Servings: 4

Ingredients:
- ❖ 8 ounces smoked salmon fillet, thinly sliced
- ❖ 1/2 cup cream cheese 1 medium onion, thinly sliced
- ❖ 4 bagels (about 80g each), split
- ❖ 2 tablespoons fresh parsley, chopped
- ❖ Freshly ground black pepper, to taste

Directions:
1. Spread the cream cheese on each bottom's half of bagels.
2. Top with salmon and onion, season with pepper, sprinkle with parsley, and then cover with bagel tops.
3. Serve and enjoy.

Nutritional Information:
- ❖ Calories: 309
- ❖ Fat 14.1 g
- ❖ Carbohydrates 32.0 g
- ❖ Protein 14.7 g

GREEK BAKLAVA

Preparation Time: 20 minutes
Cooking Time: 20 minutes
Servings: 18

Ingredients:
- ❖ 1 package phyllo dough
- ❖ 1 lb. chopped nuts
- ❖ 1 cup butter
- ❖ 1 teaspoon ground cinnamon
- ❖ 1 cup of water
- ❖ 1 cup white sugar
- ❖ 1 teaspoon. vanilla extract
- ❖ 1/2 cup honey

Directions:
1. Warm oven to 175°C or 350°Fahrenheit.
2. Spread butter on the sides and bottom of a 9-in by the 13-in pan.
3. Chop the nuts, then mix with cinnamon; set it aside.
4. Unfurl the phyllo dough, then halve the whole stack to fit the pan.
5. Use a damp cloth to cover the phyllo to prevent drying as you proceed.
6. Put two phyllo sheets in the pan, then butter well. Repeat to make eight layered phyllo sheets.
7. Scatter 2-3 tablespoons of the nut mixture over the sheets Place two more phyllo sheets on top; butter, then sprinkle with nuts.
8. Layer as you go. The final layer should be six to eight phyllo sheets deep.
9. Make square or diamond shapes with a sharp knife up to the bottom of the pan.
10. You can slice into four long rows for diagonal shapes. Bake until crisp and golden for 50 minutes.
11. Meanwhile, boil water and sugar until the sugar melts to make the sauce; mix in honey and vanilla.
12. Let it simmer for 20 minutes.
13. Take the baklava out of the oven, then drizzle with sauce right away; cool.
14. Serve the baklava in cupcake papers.
15. You can also freeze them without cover.
16. The baklava will turn soggy when wrapped.

Nutritional Information:
- ❖ Calories: 393
- ❖ Carbohydrate: 37.5 g
- ❖ Fat: 25.9 g

SMOKED SALMON AND CHEESE ON RYE BREAD

Preparation Time: 15 minutes
Cooking Time: 10 minutes
Servings: 4

Ingredients:
- ❖ 8 ounces smoked salmon, thinly sliced
- ❖ 1/3 cup mayonnaise
- ❖ 2 tablespoons lemon juice
- ❖ 1 tablespoon Dijon mustard
- ❖ 1 teaspoon garlic, minced
- ❖ 4 slices cheddar cheese
- ❖ 8 slices rye bread
- ❖ 8 Romaine lettuce leaves
- ❖ Salt and freshly ground black pepper

Directions:
1. Mix the mayonnaise, lemon juice, mustard, and garlic in a small bowl.
2. Flavor with salt plus pepper and set aside.
3. Spread dressing on 4 bread slices.
4. Top with lettuce, salmon, and cheese.
5. Cover with remaining rye bread slices.
6. Serve and enjoy.

Nutritional Information:
- ❖ Calories: 365
- ❖ Fat: 16.6 g
- ❖ Carbohydrates: 31.6 g
- ❖ Protein: 18.8 g

STUFFED AVOCADO

Preparation Time: 10 minutes
Cooking Time: 0 minute
Servings: 2

Ingredients:
- ❖ 1 avocado, halved and pitted
- ❖ 10 ounces of canned tuna, drained
- ❖ 2 tablespoons sun-dried tomatoes, chopped
- ❖ 1 and ½ tablespoon basil pesto
- ❖ 2 tablespoons black olives, pitted and chopped
- ❖ Salt and black pepper to the taste
- ❖ 2 teaspoons pine nuts, toasted and chopped
- ❖ 1 tablespoon basil, chopped

Directions:
1. In a bowl, mix the tuna plus sun-dried tomatoes and the rest of the ingredients except the avocado and stir.
2. Stuff the avocado halves with the tuna mix and serve as an appetizer.

Nutritional Information:
- ❖ Calories 233
- ❖ Fat 9 g
- ❖ Carbs 11.4 g
- ❖ Protein 5.6 g

HUMMUS WITH GROUND LAMB

Preparation Time: 10 minutes
Cooking Time: 15 minutes
Servings: 8

Ingredients:
- ❖ 10 ounces hummus
- ❖ 12 ounces lamb meat, ground
- ❖ ½ cup pomegranate seeds
- ❖ ¼ cup parsley, chopped
- ❖ 1 tablespoon olive oil Pita chips for serving

Directions:
1. Heat-up pan with the oil over medium-high heat, add the meat, and brown for 15 minutes, stirring often.
2. Spread the hummus on a platter, spread the ground lamb all over, also spread the pomegranate seeds and the parsley, and serve with pita chips as a snack.

Nutritional Information:
- ❖ Calories 133
- ❖ Fat 9.7 g
- ❖ Carbs 6.4 g
- ❖ Protein 5 g

WRAPPED PLUMS

Preparation Time: 5 minutes
Cooking Time: 0 minutes
Servings: 8

Ingredients:
- ❖ 2 ounces prosciutto, cut into 16 pieces
- ❖ 4 plums, quartered 1 tablespoon chives, chopped
- ❖ A pinch of red pepper flakes, crushed

Directions:
1. Wrap each plum quarter in a prosciutto slice, arrange them all on a platter, sprinkle the chives and pepper flakes all over, and serve.

Nutritional Information:
- ❖ Calories 30
- ❖ Fat 1 g
- ❖ Carbs 4 g
- ❖ Protein 2 g

VEGGIE FRITTERS

Preparation Time: 10 minutes
Cooking Time: 10 minutes
Servings: 4

Ingredients:
- ❖ 2 garlic cloves, minced
- ❖ 2 yellow onions, chopped
- ❖ 4 scallions, chopped
- ❖ 2 carrots, grated
- ❖ 2 teaspoons cumin, ground
- ❖ ½ teaspoon turmeric powder
- ❖ Salt and black pepper to the taste
- ❖ ¼ teaspoon coriander, ground
- ❖ 2 tablespoons parsley, chopped
- ❖ ¼ teaspoon lemon juice
- ❖ ½ cup almond flour
- ❖ 2 beets, peeled and grated
- ❖ 2 eggs, whisked
- ❖ ¼ cup tapioca flour
- ❖ 3 tablespoons olive oil

Directions:
1. In a bowl, combine the garlic, onions, scallions, and the rest of the ingredients except the oil, stir well and shape medium fritters out of this mix.
2. Heat oil in a pan over medium-high heat, add the fritters, cook for 5 minutes on each side, arrange on a platter and serve.

Nutritional Information:
- ❖ Calories 209
- ❖ Fat 11.2 g
- ❖ Carbs 4.4 g
- ❖ Protein 4.8 g

WHITE BEAN DIP

Preparation Time: 10 minutes
Cooking Time: 0 minute
Servings: 4

Ingredients:
- ❖ 15 oz white beans, drained & rinsed
- ❖ 6 ounces canned artichoke hearts, drained and quartered
- ❖ 4 garlic cloves, minced
- ❖ 1 tablespoon basil, chopped
- ❖ 2 tablespoons olive oil Juice of ½ lemon Zest of ½ lemon, grated
- ❖ Salt and black pepper to the taste

Directions:
1. In your food processor, combine the beans, artichokes, and the rest of the ingredients except the oil and pulse well.
2. Add the oil gradually, pulse the mix again, divide into cups, and serve as a party dip.

Nutritional Information:
- ❖ Calories 274
- ❖ Fat 11.7 g
- ❖ Carbs 18.5 g
- ❖ Protein 16.5 g

EGGPLANT DIP

Preparation Time: 10 minutes
Cooking Time: 40 minutes
Servings: 4

Ingredients:
- ❖ 1 eggplant, poked with a fork
- ❖ 2 tablespoons tahini paste
- ❖ 2 tablespoons lemon juice
- ❖ 2 garlic cloves, minced
- ❖ 1 tablespoon olive oil
- ❖ Salt and black pepper to the taste
- ❖ 1 tablespoon parsley, chopped

Directions:
1. Put the eggplant in a roasting pan, bake at 400° F for 40 minutes, cool down, peel and transfer to your food processor.
2. Add the remaining ingredients except for the parsley, pulse well, divide into small bowls and serve as an appetizer with the parsley sprinkled on top.

Nutritional Information:
- ❖ Calories 121
- ❖ Fat 4.3 g
- ❖ Carbs 1.4 g
- ❖ Protein 4.3 g 231.

CUCUMBER ROLLS

Preparation Time: 5 minutes
Cooking Time: 0 minutes
Servings: 6

Ingredients:
- ❖ 1 big cucumber, sliced lengthwise
- ❖ 1 tablespoon parsley, chopped
- ❖ 8 ounces canned tuna, drained and mashed
- ❖ Salt and black pepper to the taste
- ❖ 1 teaspoon lime juice

Directions:
1. Arrange cucumber slices on a working surface, divide the rest of the ingredients, and roll.
2. Arrange all the rolls on a surface and serve.

Nutritional Information:
- ❖ Calories 200
- ❖ Fat 6 g
- ❖ Carbs 7.6 g
- ❖ Protein 3.5 g

OLIVES AND CHEESE STUFFED TOMATOES

Preparation Time: 10 minutes
Cooking Time: 0 minutes
Servings: 24

Ingredients:
- ❖ 24 cherry tomatoes, top cut off, and insides scooped out
- ❖ 2 tablespoons olive oil
- ❖ ¼ teaspoon red pepper flakes
- ❖ ½ cup feta cheese, crumbled
- ❖ 2 tablespoons black olive paste
- ❖ ¼ cup mint, torn

Directions:
1. In a bowl, mix the olives paste with the rest of the ingredients except the cherry tomatoes and whisk.
2. Stuff the cherry tomatoes with this mix, arrange them all on a platter, and serve.

Nutritional Information:
- ❖ Calories 136
- ❖ Fat 8.6 g
- ❖ Carbs 5.6 g
- ❖ Protein 5.1 g

GRILLED CHICKEN POWER BOWL WITH GREEN GODDESS DRESSING

Preparation Time: 5 Minutes
Cooking Time: 15 Minutes
Servings: 4

Ingredients:
- ❖ 1 ½ boneless, skinless chicken breasts
- ❖ ¼ teaspoon each salt & pepper
- ❖ 1 cup diced or cubed kabocha squash
- ❖ 1 cup diced zucchini
- ❖ 1 cup diced yellow summer squash
- ❖ 1 cup diced broccoli
- ❖ 8 cherry tomatoes, halved
- ❖ 4 radishes, sliced thin
- ❖ 1 cup shredded red cabbage
- ❖ ¼ cup hemp or pumpkin seeds

Green Goddess Dressing:
- ❖ ½ cup low-fat plain Greek yogurt
- ❖ 1 cup fresh basil
- ❖ 1 clove garlic
- ❖ 4 tbsp. lemon juice
- ❖ ¼ tsp each salt & pepper

Directions:
1. Preheat oven to 350°F. Season chicken with salt and pepper.
2. Roast chicken for 12 minutes until it reaches a temperature of 165°F.
3. When done, dismiss from the oven and set aside to rest for about 5 minutes.
4. Cut into bite-sized pieces and keep warm. While the chicken is resting, steam riced kabocha squash, yellow summer squash, zucchini, and broccoli in a covered microwave-proof bowl for about 5 minutes until tender.
5. For the dressing, arrange the ingredients in a blender and puree until smooth.
6. To serve, place an equal amount of Veggie Mix into four individual bowls.
7. Add an equal amount of cherry tomatoes, radishes, and chopped cabbage to each bowl, along with a quarter of the chicken and a tablespoon of seeds.
8. Dress up. Enjoy!

Nutritional Information:
- ❖ Calories: 300;
- ❖ Protein: 43 g;
- ❖ Carbohydrate: 12 g;

BACON CHEESEBURGER

Preparation Time: 5 Minutes
Cooking Time: 15 Minutes
Servings: 4

Ingredients:
- ❖ 1-pound lean ground beef
- ❖ ¼ cup chopped yellow onion
- ❖ 1 clove garlic, minced
- ❖ 1 tablespoon yellow mustard
- ❖ 1 tablespoon Worcestershire sauce
- ❖ ½ teaspoon salt Cooking spray
- ❖ 4 ultra-thin slices of cheddar cheese, cut into 6 equal-sized rectangular pieces
- ❖ 3 pieces of turkey bacon, each cut into 8 evenly-sized rectangular pieces
- ❖ 24 dill pickle chips
- ❖ 4-6 green leaf lettuce leaves, torn into 24 small square-shaped pieces
- ❖ 12 cherry tomatoes, sliced in half

Directions:
1. Preheat oven to 400°F.
2. Combine the garlic, salt, onion, Worcestershire sauce, and beef in a medium-sized bowl, and mix well. Form mixture into 24 small meatballs.
3. Put meatballs onto a foil-lined baking sheet and cook for 12-15 minutes.
4. Leave oven on. Top every meatball with a piece of cheese, then go back to the oven until cheese melts for about 2 to 3 minutes.
5. Let meatballs cool. To assemble bites: on a toothpick, layer a cheese-covered meatball, piece of bacon, piece of lettuce, pickle chip, and a tomato half.

Nutritional Information:
- ❖ Calories 234;
- ❖ Protein 20g;
- ❖ Fat 3g
- ❖ Carbs 12g

CHEESEBURGER PIE

Preparation Time: 25 Minutes
Cooking Time: 90 Minutes
Servings: 4

Ingredients:
- 1 large spaghetti squash
- 1-pound lean ground beef
- ¼ cup diced onion
- 2 eggs
- 1/3 cup low-fat, plain Greek yogurt
- 2 tablespoon Tomato sauce
- ½ teaspoon Worcestershire sauce
- 2/3 cup reduced-fat, shredded cheddar cheese
- 2 ounces dill pickle slices
- Cooking spray

Directions:
1. Preheat oven to 400°F.
2. Slice spaghetti squash in half lengthwise; dismiss pulp and seeds.
3. Spray cooking spray.
4. Place the cut pumpkin halves on a foil-lined baking sheet and bake for 30 minutes.
5. Once cooked, let it cool before scraping the pulp from the squash with a fork to remove the spaghetti-like strings. Set aside.
6. Push squash strands in the bottom and up sides of the greased pie pan, creating an even layer.
7. Meanwhile, set up pie filling. In a lightly greased, medium-sized skillet, cook beef and onion over medium heat for 8 to 10 minutes, sometimes stirring, until meat is brown.
8. Drain and remove from heat.
9. Whisk together the eggs, tomato paste, Greek yogurt and Worcestershire sauce and add the ground beef mixture.
10. Pour the pie filling over the pumpkin rind. Sprinkle the meat filling with cheese, and then fill with pickled cucumber slices.
11. Bake for 40 minutes.

Nutritional Information:
- Calories: 270;
- Protein: 23 g;
- Carbohydrate: 10 g;
- Fat: 23 g

CRISPY APPLES

Preparation Time: 10 Minutes
Cooking Time: 10 Minutes
Servings: 4

Ingredients:
- ❖ 2 tbsp. cinnamon powder
- ❖ 5 apples
- ❖ ½ tablespoon nutmeg powder
- ❖ 1 tablespoon maple syrup
- ❖ ½ cup water
- ❖ 4 tablespoon butter
- ❖ ¼ cup flour
- ❖ ¾ cup oats
- ❖ ¼ cup brown sugar

Directions:
1. Get the apples in a pan, put in nutmeg, maple syrup, cinnamon and water.
2. Mix in butter with flour, sugar, salt and oat, turn, put a spoonful of the blend over apples, get into the air fryer and cook at 350°F for 10 minutes.
3. Serve while warm.

Nutritional Information:
- ❖ Calories: 387;
- ❖ Total Fat: 5.6g;
- ❖ Total carbs: 12.4g

TURKEY CAPRESE MEATLOAF CUPS

Preparation Time: 20 Minutes
Cooking Time: 45 Minutes
Servings: 6

Ingredients:
- ❖ 1 large egg
- ❖ 2 pounds ground turkey breast
- ❖ 3 pieces of sun-dried tomatoes, drained and chopped
- ❖ ¼ cup fresh basil leaves, chopped
- ❖ 5 ounces low-fat fresh mozzarella, shredded
- ❖ ½ teaspoon garlic powder
- ❖ ¼ teaspoon salt and
- ❖ ½ teaspoon pepper, to taste

Directions:
1. Preheat oven to 400°F. Beat the egg in a big mixing bowl.
2. Add the remaining ingredients and mix everything with your hands until evenly combined.
3. Spray a 12-cup muffin tin and divide the turkey mixture among the muffin cups, pressing the mix in. Cook in the preheated oven till the turkey is well-cooked for about 25-30 minutes.
4. Chill the meatloaves entirely and store them in a container in the fridge for up to 5 days.

Nutritional Information:
- ❖ Calories 181;
- ❖ Protein 43g;
- ❖ Fat 11;
- ❖ Carbs 9

ZUCCHINI MUFFINS

Preparation Time: 10 minutes
Cooking Time: 25 minutes
Servings: 16

Ingredients:
- ❖ 1 tablespoon ground flaxseed
- ❖ 3 tablespoons. alkaline water
- ❖ ¼ cup walnut butter
- ❖ 3 medium over-ripe bananas
- ❖ 2 small grated zucchinis
- ❖ 1/2 cup coconut milk
- ❖ 1 teaspoon vanilla extract
- ❖ 2 cups coconut flour
- ❖ 1 tablespoon baking powder
- ❖ 1 teaspoon cinnamon
- ❖ 1/4 teaspoon sea salt

Directions:
1. Tune the temperature of your oven to 375°F.
2. Grease the muffin tray with the cooking spray.
3. In a bowl, mix the flaxseed with water.
4. In a glass bowl, mash the bananas, then stir in the remaining ingredients.
5. Properly mix and then divide the mixture into the muffin tray.
6. Bake it for 25 minutes.
7. Serve.

Nutritional Information:
- ❖ Calories: 127 kcal;
- ❖ Fat: 6.6g;
- ❖ Carbs: 13g;
- ❖ Protein: 0.7g

WHOLE-WHEAT BLUEBERRY MUFFINS

Preparation Time: 5 Minutes
Cooking Time: 25 Minutes
Servings: 8

Ingredients:
- ❖ 1/2 cup plant-based milk
- ❖ 1/2 cup unsweetened applesauce
- ❖ 1/2 cup maple syrup
- ❖ 1 teaspoon vanilla extract
- ❖ 2 cups whole-wheat flour
- ❖ 1/2 teaspoon baking soda
- ❖ 1 cup blueberries

Directions:
1. Preheat the oven to 375°F.
2. In a large bowl, mix the milk, applesauce, maple syrup, and vanilla.
3. Stir in the flour and baking soda until no dry flour is left, and the batter is smooth.
4. Gently fold in the blueberries until they are evenly distributed throughout the batter.
5. In a muffin tin, fill 8 muffin cups three-quarters full of batter.
6. Bake for 25 minutes, or until you can stick a knife into the center of a muffin and it comes out clean.
7. Allow cooling before serving.

Nutritional Information:
- ❖ Fat: 1 g;
- ❖ Carbohydrates: 45 g;
- ❖ Fiber: 2 g;
- ❖ Protein: 4 g

WALNUT CRUNCH BANANA BREAD

Preparation Time: 5 Minutes
Cooking Time: 1 Hour and 30 Minutes
Servings: 1

Ingredients:
- ❖ 4 ripe bananas
- ❖ 1/4 cup maple syrup
- ❖ 1 tablespoon apple cider vinegar
- ❖ 1 teaspoon vanilla extract
- ❖ 11/2 cups whole-wheat flour
- ❖ 1/2 teaspoon ground cinnamon
- ❖ 1/2 teaspoon baking soda
- ❖ 1/4 cup walnut pieces (optional)

Directions:
1. Preheat the oven to 350°F.
2. In a large bowl, use a fork or mixing spoon to mash the bananas until they reach a puréed consistency (small bits of banana are acceptable). Stir in the maple syrup, apple cider vinegar, and vanilla.
3. Stir in the flour, cinnamon, and baking soda.
4. Fold in the walnut pieces (if using).
5. Gently pour the batter into a loaf pan, filling it no more than three-quarters of the way full.
6. Bake for 1 hour, or until you can stick a knife into the middle and it comes out clean.
7. Transfer from the oven then let cooling on the countertop for a minimum of 30 minutes before serving.

Nutritional Information:
- ❖ Fat: 1g;
- ❖ Carbohydrates: 40 g;
- ❖ Fiber: 5 g;
- ❖ Protein: 4 g

CARROT STICKS WITH AVOCADO DIP

Preparation time: ten minutes
Cooking time 0 minutes
Servings 6

Ingredients:
- ½ cup cilantro, firmly packed
- ½ onion
- 1 big avocado, pitted
- 1 tablespoon of chili-garlic sauce or chili sauce 2 tablespoon olive oil
- 6 ounces shelled edamame
- Juice of one lemon
- Salt and pepper

Directions:
1. Put the edamame, cilantro, onion, and chili sauce in a blender or food processor.
2. Pulse it to cut and mix the ingredients.
3. Put in the avocado and the lemon juice.
4. Slowly put in the olive oil as you blend.
5. Move to a jar.
6. Scoop 2 spoons and serve with carrot sticks.

Nutritional Information:
- Calories: 154 kcal
- Protein: 5.16 g
- Fat: 11.96 g
- Carbohydrates: 8.44 g

THE CASHEW "HUMUS"

Preparation time: ten minutes
Cooking time: 0 minutes
Servings 1

Ingredients:
- ¼ Cup Water
- ¼ Teaspoon
- Sea Salt, Fine
- ½ Teaspoon Ground Ginger
- 1 Cup Cashews, Raw & Soaked in Water for fifteen Minutes & Drained
- 1 Tablespoon Olive Oil
- 1 Teaspoon Lemon juice, Fresh
- 2 Cloves Garlic
- 2 Teaspoon Coconut Aminos Pinch Cayenne Pepper

Directions:
1. Blend all ingredients together, and ensure to scrape the sides.
2. Continue to combine until the desired smoothness is achieved, and then place in your fridge it before you serve.

Nutritional Information:
- Calories: 112
- Protein: 2.9
- Fat: 8.8

GRAMS CASHEW CHEESE

Preparation time: 2 hours
Cooking time 0 minutes
Servings 6

Ingredients:
- ❖ ¼ cup of fresh basil
- ❖ 1 cup of raw cashews
- ❖ 1 tablespoon of Nutritional Informational yeast
- ❖ Juice of ½ lemon
- ❖ Salt and pepper to taste

Directions:
1. In a1 cup of water, soak the cashew for minimum 2 hours. Drain.
2. Put the cashews, lemon juice, Nutritional Informational yeast, and fresh basil into a food processor and pulse until the desired smoothness is achieved.
3. Put in 1 tablespoon of water at a time to make it creamy, but not runny.
4. Flavor it with pepper and salt, then spread it on gluten-free bread or toast.
5. Store in an airtight jar in your fridge.

Nutritional Information:
- ❖ Total Carbohydrates: 126g
- ❖ Fiber: 1g
- ❖ Protein: 4g
- ❖ Total Fat: 10g ‖
- ❖ Calories: 126

CAULIFLOWER SNACKS

Preparation time: ten minutes
Cooking time: 60 minutes Yield:
Servings 4

Ingredients:
- ❖ 1 head of cauliflower
- ❖ 1 teaspoon salt
- ❖ 4 tablespoons extra virgin olive oil

Directions:
1. Set the oven to 425F, then prepare two cookie sheets by lining them using parchment paper.
2. Trim off the cauliflower florets and discard the core.
3. Chop the florets into golf-ball-sized pieces.
4. Put the cauliflower in a container, and pour olive oil over them and drizzle with salt. Mix to coat.
5. Spread in a single layer, not touching.
6. Roast approximately 1 hour flipping the cauliflower three to four times until a golden-brown color is achieved.

Nutritional Information:
- ❖ Calories: 91 kcal
- ❖ Protein: 2.93 g
- ❖ Fat: 7.7 g
- ❖ Carbohydrates: 3.29 g

SPICY ROASTED CHICKPEAS

Preparation time: ten minutes
Cooking time: forty minutes
Servings 6

Ingredients:
- ❖ ¼ teaspoon of cayenne pepper
- ❖ 1 teaspoon of paprika
- ❖ 1 teaspoon of turmeric
- ❖ 2 (fifteen ounce) cans of chickpeas, drained and washed
- ❖ 2 teaspoons of coconut oil, melted

Directions:
1. Set the oven to 425°F.
2. Coat a baking sheet using a paper towels, then put the chickpeas on them and use more paper towels to take off the surplus water in the chickpeas.
3. Remove all of the paper towels.
4. Place the oil and spices to the chickpeas and mix thoroughly.
5. Roast your chickpeas for forty minutes, stirring every ten minutes.
6. Once the chickpeas are done, take it off from the oven and let fully cool.

Nutritional Information:
- ❖ Total Carbohydrates: 19g
- ❖ Fiber: 6g
- ❖ Protein: 7g
- ❖ Total Fat: 4g
- ❖ Calories: 138

SWEET POTATO MUFFINS

Preparation time: fifteen minutes
Cooking time: 20-twenty-five minutes
 Servings 12

Ingredients:
- ¼ Cup Almond Butter
- ¼ Teaspoon Sea Salt
- ½ Teaspoon Baking Soda
- 1 ½ Cups Rolled Oats
- 1 Cup Almond Milk
- 1 Cup Sweet Potato, Cooked & Pureed
- 1 Egg
- 1 Teaspoon Baking Powder
- 1 Teaspoon Ground Cinnamon
- 1 Teaspoon Vanilla Extract, Pure
- 1/3 Cup Coconut Sugar
- 2 Tablespoons Olive Oil

Directions:
1. Begin by heating the oven to 375.
2. Coat your muffin tin with liners, and get out a food processor.
3. Pulse your oats until it forms a course flour. Move it to a small container before setting it to the side.
4. Put in all of your ingredients apart from for the oat flour, blending until the desired smoothness is achieved.
5. Slowly put in in your oat flour, pulsing until it's well blended.
6. Cut between your cupcake liners, and bake for about twenty minutes.
7. Let them cool for minimum five minutes before you serve.

Nutritional Information:
- Calories: 143
- Protein: 4
- Fat: 7
- Carbohydrates: 12

GRAMS SWEET SUNUP SEEDS

Preparation time: five minutes
Cooking time: 60 minutes
Servings 8

Ingredients:
- ¼-cup pure maple syrup
- ¼-cup sunflower oil
- ¼-sesame seeds
- ⅓ -cup honey
- ½-cup flaxseed
- 1-cup dried cranberries
- 1-cup raw pumpkin seeds
- 1-tsp vanilla extract
- 3-tsp cinnamon
- 4-cups rolled oats

Directions:
1. Preheat your oven to 350°F.
2. Prepare two units of baking sheets by lining them using parchment paper.
3. In a large-sized mixing container, mix the rolled oats, pumpkin seeds, flaxseed, sesame seeds, and cinnamon. Mix gently until meticulously blended.
4. Pour all the liquid ingredients into the mixture and stir until mixed well.
5. On the baking sheets, spread the mixture uniformly.
6. Place the sheets in your oven.
7. Cook for minimum an hour.
8. While baking, stir the mixture every quarter of an hour to achieve uniform color on its surfaces.
9. Take away the sheets from the oven.
10. Allow cooling completely. Put in the cup of dried cranberries, and mix thoroughly. Store the granola in an airtight container to maintain its freshness and crunchiness.

Nutritional Information:
- Calories: 189
- Fat: 6.3g
- Protein: 9.4g
- Sodium: 5mg
- Total Carbohydrates: 27.6g
- Fiber: 4g
- Net Carbohydrates: 23.6g

TANGY TURMERIC FLAVORED FLORETS

Preparation time: ten minutes
Cooking time: 55 minutes
Servings 1

Ingredients:
- ❖ 1-head cauliflower, chopped into florets
- ❖ 1-Tbsp olive oil
- ❖ 1-Tbsp turmeric
- ❖ A dash of salt
- ❖ A pinch of cumin

Directions:
1. Set the oven to 400°F.
2. Combine all ingredients in a baking pan.
3. Mix thoroughly until meticulously blended.
4. Cover the pan using foil. Roast for forty minutes.
5. Take away the foil cover and roast additionally for fifteen minutes.

Nutritional Information:
- ❖ Calories: 90
- ❖ Fat: 3g
- ❖ Protein: 4.5g
- ❖ Sodium: 87mg
- ❖ Total Carbohydrates: 16.2g
- ❖ Fiber: 5g
- ❖ Net Carbohydrates: 11.2g

TOASTED PUMPKIN SEEDS

Preparation time: five minutes
Cooking time: thirty minutes
Servings 2-4

Ingredients:
- ❖ ½ teaspoon extra virgin olive oil
- ❖ 1 teaspoon salt
- ❖ 1 to 2 cups pumpkin seeds
- ❖ Sea salt Water

Directions:
1. Put seeds in a deep cooking pan and cover with water.
2. Put in salt.
3. Bring it to its boiling point and boil for about ten minutes.
4. Simmer uncovered for ten more minutes.
5. This makes the seeds very crunchy when baked.
6. Drain the seeds and pat dry using a paper towel.
7. Coat a baking sheet using parchment paper and spread out the seeds in a single layer.
8. Sprinkle with salt, then bake in an oven at 325F for minimum ten minutes, stirring midway through.
9. Cool, then store in an airtight container.

Nutritional Information:
- ❖ Calories: 192 kcal
- ❖ Protein: 10.41 g
- ❖ Fat: 16.23 g
- ❖ Carbohydrates: 4.34 g

CARAMELIZED PEARS AND ONIONS

Preparation time: five minutes
Cooking time: thirty-five minutes
Servings 4

Ingredients:
- ❖ 1 tablespoon olive oil
- ❖ 2 firm red pears, cored and quartered
- ❖ 2 red onion, cut into wedges
- ❖ Salt and pepper, to taste

Directions:
1. Preheat the oven to 425 degrees F
2. Put the pears and onion on a baking tray Sprinkle with olive oil
3. Sprinkle with salt and pepper
4. Bake using your oven for a little more than half an hour Serve and enjoy!

Nutritional Informational
- ❖ Calories: 101
- ❖ Fat: 4g
- ❖ Carbohydrates: 17g
- ❖ Protein: 1g

CAULIFLOWER BROCCOLI MASH

Preparation time: five minutes
Cooking time: ten minutes
Servings 6

Ingredients:
- ❖ 1 big head cauliflower, cut into chunks
- ❖ 1 small head broccoli, cut into florets
- ❖ 1 teaspoon salt
- ❖ 3 tablespoons extra virgin olive oil Pepper, to taste

Directions:
1. Take a pot and put in oil then heat it
2. Put in the cauliflower and broccoli
3. Sprinkle with salt and pepper to taste
4. Keep stirring to make vegetable soft
5. Put in water if required
6. When is already cooked, use a food processor or a potato masher to puree the vegetables
7. Serve and enjoy!

Nutritional Information:
- ❖ Calories: 39
- ❖ Fat: 3g
- ❖ Carbohydrates: 2g
- ❖ Protein: 0.89g

CILANTRO AND AVOCADO PLATTER

Preparation time: ten minutes
Cooking time: 0 minutes
 Servings 6

Ingredients:
- ❖ ¼ cup of fresh cilantro, chopped
- ❖ ½ a lime, juiced
- ❖ 1 big ripe tomato, chopped
- ❖ 1 green bell pepper, chopped
- ❖ 1 sweet onion, chopped
- ❖ 2 avocados, peeled, pitted and diced
- ❖ Salt and pepper as required

Directions:
1. Take a moderate-sized container and put in onion, bell pepper, tomato, avocados, lime and cilantro
2. Mix thoroughly and give it a toss
3. Sprinkle with salt and pepper in accordance with your taste
4. Serve and enjoy!

Nutritional Information:
- ❖ Calories: 126
- ❖ Fat: 10g
- ❖ Carbohydrates: 10g
- ❖ Protein: 2g

CITRUS COUSCOUS WITH HERB

Preparation time: five minutes
Cooking time: fifteen minutes
Servings 2

Ingredients:
- ¼ cup of water
- ¼ orange, chopped
- ½ teaspoon butter
- 1 teaspoon Italian seasonings
- 1/3 cup couscous
- 1/3 teaspoon salt
- 4 tablespoons orange juice

Directions:
1. Pour water and orange juice in the pan.
2. Put in orange, Italian seasoning, and salt.
3. Bring the liquid to boil and take it off the heat.
4. Put in butter and couscous. Stir thoroughly and close the lid.
5. Leave the couscous rest for about ten minutes.

Nutritional Information:
- Calories 149
- Fat: 1.9
- Fiber: 2.1
- Carbs: 28.5
- Protein: 4.1

COOL GARBANZO AND SPINACH BEANS

Preparation time: 5-ten minutes
Cooking time: 0 minute
Servings 4

Ingredients:
- ❖ ½ onion, diced
- ❖ ½ teaspoon cumin
- ❖ 1 tablespoon olive oil
- ❖ 10 ounces spinach, chopped
- ❖ 12 ounces garbanzo beans

Directions:
1. Take a frying pan and put in olive oil
2. Put it on moderate to low heat
3. Put in onions, garbanzo and cook for five minutes
4. Mix in cumin, garbanzo beans, spinach and flavor with sunflower seeds
5. Use a spoon to smash gently
6. Cook meticulously
7. Serve and enjoy!

Nutritional Information:
- ❖ Calories: 90
- ❖ Fat: 4g
- ❖ Carbohydrates:11g
- ❖ Protein:4g

CRISPY CORN

Preparation time: 8 minutes
Cooking time: five minutes
Servings 3

Ingredients:
- ❖ ½ teaspoon ground paprika
- ❖ ½ teaspoon salt
- ❖ ¾ teaspoon chili pepper
- ❖ 1 cup corn kernels
- ❖ 1 tablespoon coconut flour
- ❖ 1 tablespoon water
- ❖ 3 tablespoons canola oil

Directions:
1. In the mixing container, mix together corn kernels with salt and coconut flour.
2. Put in water and mix up the corn with the help of the spoon.
3. Pour canola oil in the frying pan and heat it.
4. Put in corn kernels mixture and roast it for about four minutes.
5. Stir it occasionally.
6. When the corn kernels are crispy, move them in the plate and dry with the paper towel's help.
7. Put in chili pepper and ground paprika.
8. Mix up well.

Nutritional Information:
- ❖ Calories 179
- ❖ Fat: fifteen
- ❖ Fiber: 2.4
- ❖ Carbs: 11.3
- ❖ Protein: 2.1

PARMESAN ROASTED BROCCOLI

Preparation time: ten minutes
Cooking time: twenty minutes
Servings 6

Ingredients:
- ❖ ½ teaspoon of Italian seasoning
- ❖ 1 tablespoon of lemon juice
- ❖ 1 tablespoon parsley, chopped
- ❖ 3 tablespoons of olive oil
- ❖ 3 tablespoons of vegan parmesan, grated
- ❖ 4 cups of broccoli florets
- ❖ Pepper and salt to taste

Directions:
1. Preheat the oven to 450 degrees F.
2. Apply cooking spray on your pan.
3. Keep the broccoli florets in a freezer bag.
4. Now put in the Italian seasoning, olive oil, pepper, and salt.
5. Seal your bag.
6. Shake it.
7. Coat well.
8. Pour your broccoli on the pan.
9. It must be in a single layer.
10. Bake for about twenty minutes.
11. Stir midway through.
12. Take out from the oven.
13. Drizzle parsley and parmesan.
14. Sprinkle some lemon juice.
15. You can decorate with lemon wedges if you wish.

Nutritional Information:
- ❖ Calories 96
- ❖ Carbohydrates: 4g
- ❖ Cholesterol: 2mg
- ❖ Total Fat: 8g
- ❖ Protein: 2g
- ❖ Sugar: 1g
- ❖ Fiber: 1g
- ❖ Sodium: 58mg
- ❖ Potassium: 191mg

SPICED SWEET POTATO BREAD

Preparation time: fifteen minutes
Cooking time: 45-55 minutes
Servings 2

Ingredients:
For dry Ingredients:
- ❖ ¼ teaspoon sea salt
- ❖ 1 cup coconut flour
- ❖ 1 teaspoon ground mace
- ❖ 2 tablespoons ground cinnamon
- ❖ 2 teaspoons baking powder
- ❖ 2 teaspoons baking soda
- ❖ 2 teaspoons ground nutmeg

Wet Ingredients:
- ❖ 1 cup almond butter
- ❖ 2 teaspoons organic almond extract
- ❖ 4 big sweet potatoes, peeled, thinly cut
- ❖ 4 tablespoons coconut oil
- ❖ 8 big eggs
- ❖ 8 tablespoons melted grass fed butter, unsalted

Directions:
1. Grease 2 loaf pans of 9 x 5 inches with coconut oil.
2. Coat the bottom of the pan using parchment paper. Set aside.
3. Put a medium deep cooking pan on moderate heat.
4. Put in sweet potatoes.
5. Pour enough water to immerse the sweet potatoes.
6. Cook until the sweet potatoes are soft.
7. Remove the heat and drain the sweet potatoes.
8. Put in the sweet potatoes back into the pan.
9. Mash with a potato masher until the desired smoothness is achieved.
10. Allow it to cool completely.
11. Put all together the dry ingredients into a container and mix thoroughly.
12. Put in eggs into a big container and whisk well.
13. Put in sweet potatoes, butter, almond extract and almond butter and whisk until well blended.
14. Put in the dry ingredients into the container of wet ingredients and whisk until well blended.
15. Split the batter into the prepared loaf pans.

16. Bake in a preheated oven at 350°F for approximately 45 -55 minutes or a toothpick when inserted in the middle of the loaf comes out clean.
17. Remove from oven and cool to room temperature.
18. Slice using a sharp knife into slices of 1-inch thickness.

Nutritional Information:
- ❖ Calories: 1738 kcal
- ❖ Protein: 27 g
- ❖ Fat: 145.92 g
- ❖ Carbohydrates: 89.58 g

SPINACH-MUSHROOM FRITTATA

Preparation time: 15 m
Cooking time: 30 m
 Serving: 2

Ingredients:
- ❖ 10 ounce frozen chopped spinach, thawed
- ❖ 4 eggs
- ❖ 1 cup carrot, diced
- ❖ ½ cup grape tomatoes, diced
- ❖ ¾ cup Portobello mushrooms, chopped
- ❖ ½ cup scallions, finely chopped
- ❖ 1 teaspoon garlic powder
- ❖ ½ teaspoon dried oregano
- ❖ ¼ teaspoon dried rosemary
- ❖ ¼ teaspoon thyme
- ❖ ½ teaspoon unrefined sea salt
- ❖ 1 pinch ground black pepper
- ❖ Olive oil for greasing

Directions:
1. Preheat your oven to 375°F.
2. Meanwhile grease a medium size pie plate with olive oil.
3. Add all the ingredients to the pie plate and mix them thoroughly.
4. Place the pie plate in the oven and bake for 30-32 minutes or until set.
5. Remove the plate from the oven and let it cool for some time.
6. Slice into wedges and serve warm.

Nutritional Information:
- ❖ Calories 120
- ❖ Fat 3g
- ❖ Protein 3g
- ❖ Carbohydrates 21g
- ❖ Fiber 1g
- ❖ Cholesterol 0mg
- ❖ Sodium 300mg

SMOKED SALMON FRITTATA

Servings: 4

Ingredients:
- ❖ 4 tablespoons olive oil
- ❖ ½ teaspoon of garlic
- ❖ 2 medium shallots, chopped
- ❖ ½ teaspoon unrefined sea salt
- ❖ ¼ teaspoon ground black pepper
- ❖ 4 ounces pepper smoked salmon
- ❖ 4 red bell peppers, seeded and chopped
- ❖ 6 pasture-fed eggs 2 tablespoons pure coconut milk
- ❖ ¼ teaspoon dried oregano
- ❖ ½ teaspoon dried rosemary
- ❖ 1 teaspoon fresh dill, chopped

Directions:
1. Let your oven heat up to 350°F (175°C).
2. Take an oven-safe skillet and heat olive oil at medium heat in it.
3. Add garlic to the skillet and cook until the garlic becomes lightly browned.
4. Add the shallots, salt and pepper to the skillet and cook until the shallots become translucent.
5. Now, stir in the salmon and red bell pepper and cook for about 5-6 minutes.
6. Meanwhile, in a large bowl, whisk together the eggs, coconut milk, oregano, rosemary and dill.
7. Pour this mixture over the salmon in the skillet and cook for another 5 minutes or until the eggs become set.
8. Finally, place the skillet in the oven. Bake until the salmon becomes golden brown (15-18 minutes).
9. Remove the skillet from the oven and cut it into wedges before serving.

Nutritional Information:
- ❖ Calories 362
- ❖ Fat 29.4g
- ❖ Protein 16.1g
- ❖ Carbohydrates 10.5g
- ❖ Fiber 2.8g
- ❖ Cholesterol 264mg
- ❖ Sodium 511mg

BACON-WRAPPED ASPARAGUS WITH BROWN RICE

Servings: 4

Ingredients:

For Bacon-wrapped Asparagus:
- ❖ 1 pound asparagus, ends trimmed
- ❖ 12 slices nitrite/nitrate-free bacon
- ❖ 2 tablespoons grass-fed raw milk butter
- ❖ 1 tablespoon Dijon mustard 4 cloves garlic, chopped

For Brown Rice:
- ❖ 1 cup long-grain gluten-free brown rice
- ❖ 2 cups water
- ❖ ½ teaspoon unrefined sea salt

Directions:
1. Let our oven heat up to 425°F (220°C).
2. Meanwhile, rinse the brown rice thoroughly in cold water.
3. Take a medium saucepan and add water to it.
4. Boil the water at high heat and add brown rice and salt.
5. Now, reduce the heat to low and cover the saucepan.
6. Simmer the rice until it becomes tender (about 50 minutes).
7. Remove the saucepan from the heat and let it sit for another 10-12 minutes, covered.
8. Now, take a baking sheet and line it with aluminum foil.
9. Take the asparagus and rub each piece with butter.
10. Then, make bundles of 3 asparagus each to get 12 bundles.
11. Roll one slice of bacon around one bundle of asparagus.
12. Sprinkle mustard and garlic over it. Repeat this for all 12 bundles.
13. Place the bacon wrapped asparagus in the oven and bake until the bacon becomes crispy (about 25 minutes).
14. Remove from the oven and your roasted bacon-wrapped asparagus is ready to be served over brown rice.

Nutritional Information:
- ❖ Calories 320
- ❖ Fat 12.6g
- ❖ Protein 10.5g
- ❖ Carbohydrates 41.5g
- ❖ Fiber 4.1g
- ❖ Cholesterol 15mg
- ❖ Sodium 350mg

HERBED PANINI FILLET O'FISH

Preparation time: 15 minutes
Cooking time: 25 minutes
Servings: 4

Ingredients:
- ❖ 4 slices thick sourdough bread
- ❖ 4 slices mozzarella cheese
- ❖ 1 portabella mushroom, sliced
- ❖ 1 small onion, sliced
- ❖ 6 tbsp oil
- ❖ 4 garlic and herb fish fillets

Directions:
1. Prepare your fillets by adding salt, pepper, and herbs (rosemary, thyme, parsley, whatever you like).
2. Then mix in the flour before deep frying in boiling oil.
3. Once nicely browned, remove from oil and set aside.
4. On medium-high fire, sauté for five minutes the onions and mushroom in a skillet with 2 tbsp oil.
5. Prepare sourdough bread by layering the following: cheese, fish fillet, onion mixture, and cheese again before covering with another bread slice.
6. Grill in your Panini press until cheese is melted and bread is crisped and ridged.

Nutritional Information:
- ❖ Calories: 422
- ❖ Carbs: 13.2g
- ❖ Protein: 51.2g
- ❖ Fat: 17.2g

ITALIAN FLAT BREAD GLUTEN-FREE

Preparation time: 15 minutes
Cooking time: 30 minutes
Servings: 8

Ingredients:
- ❖ 1 tbsp apple cider
- ❖ 2 tbsp water
- ❖ ½ cup yogurt
- ❖ 2 tbsp butter
- ❖ 2 tbsp sugar
- ❖ 2 eggs
- ❖ 1 tsp xanthan gum
- ❖ ½ tsp salt
- ❖ 1 tsp baking soda
- ❖ 1 ½ tsp baking powder
- ❖ ½ cup potato starch, not potato flour
- ❖ ½ cup tapioca flour
- ❖ ¼ cup brown rice flour
- ❖ 1/3 cup sorghum flour

Directions:
1. With parchment paper, line an 8 x 8-inch baking pan and grease parchment paper. Preheat oven to 375oF.
2. Mix xanthan gum, salt, baking soda, baking powder, all flours, and starch in a large bowl.
3. Whisk well sugar and eggs in a medium bowl until creamed.
4. Add vinegar, water, yogurt, and butter.
5. Whisk thoroughly.
6. Pour in the egg mixture into a bowl of flours and mix well.
7. Transfer sticky dough into prepared pan and bake in the oven for 25 to 30 minutes.
8. If tops of bread start to brown a lot, cover the top with foil and continue baking until done.
9. Remove from the oven and pan right away and let it cool.
10. Best served when warm.

Nutritional Information:
- ❖ Calories: 166
- ❖ Carbs: 27.8g
- ❖ Protein: 3.4g
- ❖ Fat: 4.8g

BREAKFAST PIZZA

Preparation time: 15 minutes
Cooking time: 30 minutes
Servings: 6

Ingredients:
- ❖ 2 tablespoons coconut flour
- ❖ 2 cups cauliflower, grated
- ❖ ½ teaspoon salt
- ❖ 1 tablespoon psyllium husk powder
- ❖ 4 eggs

Toppings: Avocado Smoked Salmon Herbs Olive oil Spinach

Directions:
1. Warm the oven to 360 degrees, then grease a pizza tray.
2. Mix all ingredients in a bowl, except toppings, and keep aside.
3. Pour the pizza dough onto the pan and mold it into an even pizza crust using hands.
4. Top the pizza with toppings and transfer to the oven.
5. Bake within 15 minutes until golden brown and remove from the oven to serve.

Nutritional Information:
- ❖ Calories: 454
- ❖ Carbs: 16g
- ❖ Fats: 31g
- ❖ Proteins: 22g
- ❖ Sodium: 1325mg
- ❖ Sugar: 4.4g

MINI PIZZA CRUSTS

Preparation time: 15 minutes
Cooking time: 20 minutes
Servings: 4

Ingredients:
- ❖ 1 cup coconut flour, sifted
- ❖ 8 large eggs, 5 whole eggs, and 3 egg whites
- ❖ ½ teaspoon baking powder
- ❖ Italian spices, to taste
- ❖ Salt and black pepper, to taste

For the pizza sauce:
- ❖ 2 garlic cloves, crushed
- ❖ 1 teaspoon dried basil
- ❖ ½ cup tomato sauce
- ❖ ¼ teaspoon of sea salt

Directions:
1. Warm the oven to 350 degrees F, then oiled a baking tray.
2. Mix eggs plus egg whites in a large bowl.
3. Stir in the coconut flour, baking powder, Italian spices, salt, and black pepper.
4. Make small dough balls from this mixture and press on the baking tray.
5. Transfer to the oven and bake for about 20 minutes.
6. Allow pizza bases to cool and keep aside.
7. Combine all ingredients for the pizza sauce and sit at room temperature for half an hour.
8. Spread this pizza sauce over the pizza crusts and serve.

Nutritional Information:
- ❖ Calories: 170
- ❖ Carbs: 5.7g
- ❖ Fats: 10.5g
- ❖ Proteins: 13.6g
- ❖ Sodium: 461mg
- ❖ Sugar: 2.3g

CHERRY TOMATO BRUSCHETTA

Preparation Time: 15 Minutes
Cooking Time: 0 Minutes
Servings: 4

Ingredients:
- ❖ 8 ounces assorted cherry tomatoes, halved
- ❖ 1/3 cup fresh herbs, chopped (such as basil, parsley, tarragon, dill)
- ❖ One tablespoon extra-virgin olive oil
- ❖ ¼ teaspoon kosher salt
- ❖ 1/8 teaspoon freshly ground black pepper
- ❖ ¼ cup ricotta cheese
- ❖ Four slices whole-wheat bread, toasted

Directions:
1. Combine the tomatoes, herbs, olive oil, salt, and black pepper in a medium bowl and mix gently.
2. Spread one tablespoon of ricotta cheese onto each slice of toast—spoon one-quarter of the tomato mixture onto each bruschetta.
3. If desired, garnish with more herbs.

Nutritional Information:
- ❖ Calories: 100
- ❖ Total fat: 6g
- ❖ Cholesterol: 5mg
- ❖ Total Carbohydrates: 10g
- ❖ Fiber: 2g
- ❖ Protein: 4g

ROASTED ROSEMARY OLIVES

Preparation Time: 5 Minutes
Cooking Time: 25 Minutes
Servings: 4

Ingredients:
- ❖ 1 cup mixed variety olives, pitted and rinsed
- ❖ Two tablespoons lemon juice
- ❖ One tablespoon extra-virgin olive oil
- ❖ Six garlic cloves, peeled
- ❖ Four rosemary sprigs

Directions:
1. Preheat the oven to 400°F.
2. Combine the olive oil, olives, lemon juice, and garlic in a medium bowl and mix.
3. Spread in a single layer on the prepared baking sheet.
4. Sprinkle on the rosemary—roast for 25 minutes, tossing halfway through.
5. Take away the rosemary leaves from the stem and place in a serving bowl.
6. Add the olives and mix before serving.

Nutritional Information:
- ❖ Calories: 100
- ❖ Total fat: 9g
- ❖ Cholesterol: 0mg
- ❖ Total Carbohydrates: 4g
- ❖ Protein: 0g

PORTABLE PACKED PICNIC PIECES

Preparation Time: 10 Minutes
Cooking Time: 0 Minutes
Servings: 1

Ingredients:
- ❖ 1-slice of whole-wheat bread, cut into bite-size pieces
- ❖ 10-pcs cherry tomatoes
- ❖ ¼-oz. aged cheese, sliced
- ❖ 6-pcs oil-cured olives

Directions:
1. Pack each of the ingredients in a portable container to serve you while snacking on the go.

Nutritional Information:
- ❖ Calories: 197
- ❖ Total Fats: 9g
- ❖ Fiber: 4g
- ❖ Carbohydrates: 22g
- ❖ Protein: 7g

NATURALLY NUTTY & BUTTERY BANANA BOWL

Preparation Time: 5 Minutes
Cooking Time: 0 Minutes
Servings: 4

Ingredients:
- ❖ 4-cups vanilla Greek yogurt
- ❖ 2-pcs medium-sized bananas, sliced
- ❖ ¼-cup creamy and natural peanut butter
- ❖ 1-tsp ground nutmeg
- ❖ ¼-cup flaxseed meal

Directions:
1. Divide the yogurt equally between four serving bowls.
2. Top each yogurt bowl with the banana slices.
3. Put the peanut butter inside a microwave-safe bowl.
4. Melt the peanut butter in your microwave for 40 seconds.
5. Drizzle one tablespoon of the melted peanut butter over the bananas for each bowl.
6. To serve, sprinkle over with the ground nutmeg and flax-seed meal.

Nutritional Information:
- ❖ Calories: 370
- ❖ Total Fats: 10.6g
- ❖ Fiber: 4.7g
- ❖ Carbohydrates: 47.7g
- ❖ Protein: 22.7g

REFRESHING AND SIMPLE SALAD

Finally, everything was done in the right manner.

AVOCADO CHICKEN SALAD

Preparation Time: 5 Minutes
Cooking Time: 10 Minutes
Servings: 2

Ingredients:
- ❖ 10 ounces diced cooked chicken
- ❖ ½ cup 2% Plain Greek yogurt
- ❖ 3 ounces chopped avocado
- ❖ 12 teaspoon garlic powder
- ❖ ¼ teaspoon salt
- ❖ 1/8 teaspoon pepper
- ❖ 1 tablespoon + 1 teaspoon lime juice
- ❖ ¼ cup fresh cilantro, chopped

Directions:
1. Combine all ingredients in a medium-sized bowl.
2. Refrigerate until ready to serve.
3. Cut the chicken salad in half and serve with your favorite greens.

Nutritional Information:
- ❖ Calories 265;
- ❖ Protein 35g;
- ❖ Fat 13;
- ❖ Carbs 5

COUSCOUS SALAD

Preparation time: ten minutes
Cooking time: six minutes
Servings 4

Ingredients:
- ¼ teaspoon ground black pepper
- ¾ teaspoon ground coriander
- ½ teaspoon salt
- ¼ teaspoon paprika
- ¼ teaspoon turmeric
- 1 tablespoon butter
- 2 oz. chickpeas, canned, drained
- 1 cup fresh arugula, chopped
- 2 oz. sun-dried tomatoes, chopped
- 1 oz. Feta cheese, crumbled
- 1 tablespoon canola oil
- 1/3 cup couscous
- 1/3 cup chicken stock

Directions:
1. Bring the chicken stock to boil.
2. Put in couscous, ground black pepper, ground coriander, salt, paprika, and turmeric.
3. Put in chickpeas and butter.
4. Mix the mixture well and close the lid.
5. Allow the couscous soak the hot chicken stock for about six minutes.
6. In the meantime, in the mixing container mix together arugula, sun-dried tomatoes, and Feta cheese.
7. Put in cooked couscous mixture and canola oil.
8. Mix up the salad well.

Nutritional Information:
- Calories 18 ù
- Fat: 9
- Fiber: 3.6
- Carbs: 21.1
- Protein: 6

OLIVES AND LENTILS SALAD

Preparation Time: 10 minutes
Cooking time: 0 minutes
Servings: 2

Ingredients:
- ❖ 1/3 cup canned green lentils
- ❖ 1 tablespoon olive oil
- ❖ 2 cups baby spinach
- ❖ 1 cup black olives
- ❖ 2 tablespoons sunflower seeds
- ❖ 1 tablespoon Dijon mustard
- ❖ 2 tablespoons balsamic vinegar
- ❖ 2 tablespoons olive oil

Directions:
1. Mix the lentils with the spinach, olives, and the rest of the ingredients in a salad bowl, toss and serve cold.

Nutritional Information:
- ❖ 279 Calories
- ❖ 6.5g Fat
- ❖ 12g Protein

LIME SPINACH AND CHICKPEAS SALAD

Preparation Time: 10 minutes
Cooking time: 0 minutes
Servings: 4

Ingredients:
- ❖ 16 ounces canned chickpeas
- ❖ 2 cups baby spinach leaves
- ❖ ½ tablespoon lime juice
- ❖ 2 tablespoons olive oil
- ❖ 1 teaspoon cumin, ground
- ❖ ½ teaspoon chili flakes

Directions:
1. Mix the chickpeas with the spinach and the rest of the ingredients in a large bowl, toss and serve cold.

Nutritional Information:
- ❖ 240 Calories
- ❖ 8.2g Fat
- ❖ 12g protein

MINTY OLIVES AND TOMATOES SALAD

Preparation Time: 10 minutes
Cooking time: 0 minutes
Servings: 4

Ingredients:
- ❖ 1 cup kalamata olives
- ❖ 1 cup black olives
- ❖ 1 cup cherry tomatoes
- ❖ 4 tomatoes 1 red onion, chopped
- ❖ 2 tablespoons oregano, chopped
- ❖ 1 tablespoon mint, chopped
- ❖ 2 tablespoons balsamic vinegar
- ❖ ¼ cup olive oil
- ❖ 2 teaspoons Italian herbs, dried

Directions:
1. In a salad bowl, mix the olives with the tomatoes and the rest of the ingredients, toss, and serve cold.

Nutritional Information:
- ❖ 190 Calories
- ❖ 8.1g Fat
- ❖ 4.6g Protein

BEANS AND CUCUMBER SALAD

Preparation Time: 10 minutes
Cooking time: 0 minutes
Servings: 4

Ingredients:
- ❖ 15 oz canned great northern beans
- ❖ 2 tablespoons olive oil
- ❖ ½ cup baby arugula
- ❖ 1 cup cucumber
- ❖ 1 tablespoon parsley
- ❖ 2 tomatoes, cubed
- ❖ 2 tablespoon balsamic vinegar

Directions:
1. Mix the beans with the cucumber and the rest of the ingredients in a large bowl, toss and serve cold.

Nutritional Information:
- ❖ 233 Calories
- ❖ 9g Fat
- ❖ 8g protein

TOMATO AND AVOCADO SALAD

Preparation Time: 10 minutes
Cooking time: 0 minutes
Servings: 4

Ingredients:
- ❖ 1-pound cherry tomatoes
- ❖ 2 avocados
- ❖ 1 sweet onion, chopped
- ❖ 2 tablespoons lemon juice
- ❖ 1 and ½ tablespoons olive oil
- ❖ Handful basil, chopped

Directions:
- ❖ Mix the tomatoes with the avocados and the rest of the ingredients in a serving bowl, toss and serve right away.

Nutritional Information:
- ❖ 148 Calories
- ❖ 7.8g Fat
- ❖ 5.5g Protein

ARUGULA SALAD

Preparation Time: 5 minutes
Cooking time: 0 minutes
Servings: 4

Ingredients:
- ❖ Arugula leaves (4 cups)
- ❖ Cherry tomatoes (1 cup)
- ❖ Pine nuts (.25 cup)
- ❖ Rice vinegar (1 tbsp.)
- ❖ Olive/grapeseed oil (2 tbsp.)
- ❖ Grated parmesan cheese (.25 cup)
- ❖ Black pepper & salt (as desired)
- ❖ Large sliced avocado (1)

Directions:
1. Peel and slice the avocado.
2. Rinse and dry the arugula leaves, grate the cheese, and slice the cherry tomatoes into halves.
3. Combine the arugula, pine nuts, tomatoes, oil, vinegar, salt, pepper, and cheese.
4. Toss the salad to mix and portion it onto plates with the avocado slices to serve.

Nutritional Information:
- ❖ 257 Calories
- ❖ 23g Fats
- ❖ 6.1g Protein

CHICKPEA SALAD

Preparation Time: 15 minutes
Cooking time: 0 minutes
Servings: 4

Ingredients:
- ❖ Cooked chickpeas (15 oz.)
- ❖ Diced Roma tomato (1)
- ❖ Diced green medium bell pepper (half of 1)
- ❖ Fresh parsley (1 tbsp.)
- ❖ Small white onion (1)
- ❖ Minced garlic (.5 tsp.)
- ❖ Lemon (1 juiced)

Directions:
1. Chop the tomato, green pepper, and onion.
2. Mince the garlic.
3. Combine each of the fixings into a salad bowl and toss well.
4. Cover the salad to chill for at least 15 minutes in the fridge.
5. Serve when ready.

Nutritional Information:
- ❖ 163 Calories
- ❖ 7g Fats
- ❖ 4g Protein

CHICKEN AND CABBAGE SALAD

Preparation Time: 10 minutes
Cooking time: 6 minutes
Servings: 4

Ingredients:
- ❖ 3 medium chicken breasts
- ❖ 4 ounces green cabbage
- ❖ 5 tablespoon extra-virgin olive oil
- ❖ Salt and black pepper to taste
- ❖ 2 tablespoons sherry vinegar tablespoon chives
- ❖ ¼ cup feta cheese, crumbled
- ❖ ¼ cup barbeque sauce
- ❖ Bacon slices, cooked and crumbled

Directions:
1. In a bowl, mix 4 tablespoon oil with vinegar, salt and pepper to taste and stir well.
2. Add the shredded cabbage, toss to coat, and leave aside for now.
3. Season chicken with salt and pepper, heat a pan with remaining oil over medium-high heat, add chicken, cook for 6 minutes, take off heat, transfer to a bowl and mix well with barbeque sauce.
4. Arrange salad on serving plates, add chicken strips, sprinkle cheese, chives, and crumbled bacon, and serve right away.

Nutritional Information:
- ❖ 200 Calories
- ❖ 15g Fat
- ❖ 33g Protein

ROASTED BROCCOLI SALAD

Preparation Time: 9 minutes
Cooking time: 17 minutes
Servings: 4

Ingredients:
- ❖ 1 lb. broccoli
- ❖ 3 tablespoons olive oil, divided
- ❖ 1-pint cherry tomatoes
- ❖ 1 ½ teaspoons honey
- ❖ 3 cups cubed bread, whole grain
- ❖ 1 tablespoon balsamic vinegar
- ❖ ½ teaspoon black pepper
- ❖ ¼ teaspoon sea salt, fine grated parmesan for serving

Directions:
1. Set the oven to 450, and then place a rimmed baking sheet.
2. Drizzle your broccoli with a tablespoon of oil, and toss to coat.
3. Take out from the oven, and spoon the broccoli.
4. Leave oil at the bottom of the bowl and add in your tomatoes, toss to coat, then mix tomatoes with a tablespoon of honey. place on the same baking sheet.
5. Roast for fifteen minutes, and stir halfway through your cooking time.
6. Add in your bread, and then roast for three more minutes.
7. Whisk two tablespoons of oil, vinegar, and remaining honey.
8. Season. Pour this over your broccoli mix to serve.

Nutritional Information:
- ❖ 226 Calories
- ❖ 7g Protein
- ❖ 12g Fat

TOMATO SALAD

Preparation Time: 22 minutes
Cooking time: 0 minute
Servings: 4

Ingredients:
- ❖ 1 cucumber, sliced
- ❖ ¼ cup sun-dried tomatoes, chopped
- ❖ 1 lb. tomatoes, cubed
- ❖ ½ cup black olives
- ❖ 1 red onion, sliced
- ❖ 1 tablespoon balsamic vinegar
- ❖ ¼ cup parsley, fresh & chopped
- ❖ 2 tablespoons olive oil

Directions:
1. Get out a bowl and combine all your vegetables.
2. To make your dressing mix all your seasoning, olive oil, and vinegar.
3. Toss with your salad and serve fresh.

Nutritional Information:
- ❖ 126 Calories
- ❖ 2.1g Protein
- ❖ 9.2g Fat

FETA BEET SALAD

Preparation Time: 16 minutes
Cooking time: 0 minute
Servings: 4

Ingredients:
- ❖ 6 Red Beets, Cooked & Peeled
- ❖ 3 Ounces Feta Cheese, Cubed
- ❖ 2 Tablespoons Olive Oil
- ❖ 2 Tablespoons Balsamic Vinegar

Directions:
1. Combine everything, and then serve.

Nutritional Information:
- ❖ 230 Calories
- ❖ 7.3g Protein
- ❖ 12g Fat

CHICKEN AND QUINOA SALAD

Preparation Time: 10 minutes
Cooking time: 20 minutes
Servings: 2

Ingredients:
- ❖ 2 tablespoons olive oil
- ❖ 2 ounces quinoa
- ❖ 2 ounces cherry tomatoes, cut in quarters 3 ounces sweet corn Lime juice from
- ❖ 1 lime Lime zest from 1 lime, grated
- ❖ 2 spring onions, chopped
- ❖ Small red chili pepper, chopped
- ❖ Avocado 2 ounces chicken meat

Directions:
1. Fill water in a pan, bring to a boil over medium-high heat, add quinoa, stir, and cook for 12 minutes.
2. Meanwhile, put corn in a pan, heat over medium-high heat, cook for 5 minutes, and leave aside for now.
3. Drain quinoa, transfer to a bowl, add tomatoes, corn, coriander, onions, chili, lime zest, olive oil, and salt and black pepper to taste and toss.
4. In another bowl, mix avocado with lime juice and stir well.
5. Add this to quinoa salad, and chicken, toss to coat, and serve.

Nutritional Information:
- ❖ 320 Calories
- ❖ 4g Fat
- ❖ 7g Protein

MELON SALAD

Preparation Time: 20 minutes
Cooking time: 0 minutes
Servings: 6

Ingredients:
- ¼ teaspoon sea salt
- ¼ teaspoon black pepper
- 1 tablespoon balsamic vinegar
- 1 cantaloupe
- 12 watermelons
- 2 cups mozzarella balls, fresh
- 1/3 cup basil, fresh & torn
- 2 tablespoons olive oil

Directions:
1. Spoon out balls of cantaloupe, then situate them in a colander over the bowl.
2. Using a melon baller to cut the watermelon as well Drain fruits for ten minutes, then chill the juice.
3. Wipe the bowl dry, and then place your fruit in it.
4. Mix in basil, oil, vinegar, mozzarella, and tomatoes before seasoning.
5. Gently mix and serve.

Nutritional Information:
- 218 Calories
- 10g Protein
- 13g Fat

BEAN AND TOASTED PITA SALAD

Preparation Time: 15 minutes
Cooking time: 10 minutes
Servings: 4

Ingredients:
- ❖ 3 tbsp chopped fresh mint
- ❖ 3 tbsp chopped fresh parsley
- ❖ 1 cup crumbled feta cheese
- ❖ 1 cup sliced romaine lettuce
- ❖ ½ cucumber, peeled and sliced
- ❖ 1 cup diced plum tomatoes
- ❖ 2 cups cooked pinto beans, well-drained and slightly warmed
- ❖ Pepper to taste
- ❖ 3 tbsp extra virgin olive oil
- ❖ 2 tbsp ground toasted cumin seeds
- ❖ 2 tbsp fresh lemon juice
- ❖ 1/8 tsp salt
- ❖ 2 cloves garlic, peeled
- ❖ 2 6-inch whole-wheat pita bread, cut or torn into bite-sized pieces

Directions:
1. In a large baking sheet, spread torn pita bread and bake in a preheated 400oF oven for 6 minutes.
2. With the back of a knife, mash garlic and salt until paste-like.
3. Add into a medium bowl. Whisk in ground cumin and lemon juice.
4. In a steady and slow stream, pour oil as you whisk continuously.
5. Season with pepper. In a large salad bowl, mix cucumber, tomatoes, and beans.
6. Pour in dressing, toss to coat well.
7. Add mint, parsley, feta, lettuce, and toasted pita, toss to mix once again, and serve.

Nutritional Information:
- ❖ Calories: 427
- ❖ Carbohydrates: 47.3g
- ❖ Protein: 17.7g
- ❖ Fat: 20.4g

GOAT CHEESE 'N RED BEANS SALAD

Preparation Time: 15 minutes
Cooking time: 0 minutes
Servings: 4

Ingredients:
- ❖ 2 cans of Red Kidney Beans, drained and rinsed well
- ❖ Water or vegetable broth to cover beans
- ❖ 1 bunch parsley, chopped
- ❖ 1 1/2 cups red grape tomatoes, halved
- ❖ 3 cloves garlic, minced
- ❖ 3 tablespoons olive oil
- ❖ 3 tablespoons lemon juice
- ❖ 1/2 teaspoon salt
- ❖ 1/2 teaspoon white pepper
- ❖ 6 ounces goat cheese, crumbled

Directions:
1. In a large bowl, combine beans, parsley, tomatoes, and garlic.
2. Add olive oil, lemon juice, salt, and pepper.
3. Mix well and refrigerate until ready to serve.
4. Spoon into individual dishes topped with crumbled goat cheese.

Nutritional Information:
- ❖ Calories: 385
- ❖ Carbohydrates: 44.0g
- ❖ Protein: 22.5g
- ❖ Fat: 15.0g

PEPPERS AND LENTILS SALAD

Preparation Time: 10 minutes
Cooking time: 0 minutes
Servings: 4

Ingredients:
- ❖ 14 ounces canned lentils
- ❖ 2 spring onions
- ❖ 1 red bell pepper
- ❖ 1 green bell pepper
- ❖ 1 tablespoon fresh lime juice
- ❖ 1/3 cup coriander
- ❖ 2 teaspoon balsamic vinegar

Directions:
1. In a salad bowl, combine the lentils with the onions, bell peppers, and the rest of the ingredients, toss and serve.

Nutritional Information:
- ❖ 200 Calories
- ❖ 2.45g Fat
- ❖ 5.6g Protein

CASHEWS AND RED CABBAGE SALAD

Preparation Time: 10 minutes
Cooking time: 0 minutes
Servings: 4

Ingredients:
- ❖ 1-pound red cabbage, shredded
- ❖ 2 tablespoons coriander, chopped
- ❖ ½ cup cashews halved
- ❖ 2 tablespoons olive oil
- ❖ 1 tomato, cubed
- ❖ A pinch of salt and black pepper
- ❖ 1 tablespoon white vinegar

Directions:
1. Mix the cabbage with the coriander and the rest of the ingredients in a salad bowl, toss and serve cold.

Nutritional Information:
- ❖ 210 Calories
- ❖ 6.3g Fat
- ❖ 8g Protein

APPLES AND POMEGRANATE SALAD

Preparation Time: 10 minutes
Cooking time: 0 minutes
Servings: 4

Ingredients:
- ❖ 3 big apples, cored and cubed
- ❖ 1 cup pomegranate seeds
- ❖ 3 cups baby arugula
- ❖ 1 cup walnuts, chopped
- ❖ 1 tablespoon olive oil
- ❖ 1 teaspoon white sesame seeds
- ❖ 2 tablespoons apple cider vinegar

Directions:
1. Mix the apples with the arugula and the rest of the ingredients in a bowl, toss and serve cold.

Nutritional Information:
- ❖ 160 Calories
- ❖ 4.3g Fat
- ❖ 10g Protein

CHICKPEAS, CORN AND BLACK BEANS SALAD

Preparation Time: 10 minutes
Cooking time: 0 minutes
Servings: 4

Ingredients:
- ❖ 1 and ½ cups canned black beans
- ❖ ½ teaspoon garlic powder
- ❖ 2 teaspoons chili powder
- ❖ 1 and ½ cups canned chickpeas
- ❖ 1 cup baby spinach
- ❖ 1 avocado, pitted, peeled, and chopped
- ❖ 1 cup corn kernels, chopped
- ❖ 2 tablespoons lemon juice
- ❖ 1 tablespoon olive oil
- ❖ 1 tablespoon apple cider vinegar
- ❖ 1 teaspoon chives, chopped

Directions:
1. Mix the black beans with the garlic powder, chili powder, and the rest of the ingredients in a bowl, toss and serve cold.

Nutritional Information:
- ❖ 300 Calories
- ❖ 13.4g Fat
- ❖ 13g Protein

CELERY CITRUS SALAD

Preparation Time: 15 minutes
Cooking time: 0 minutes
Servings: 6

Ingredients:
- ❖ 1 tablespoon lemon juice, fresh
- ❖ ¼ teaspoon sea salt, fine
- ❖ ¼ teaspoon black pepper 1
- ❖ tablespoon olive brine
- ❖ 1 tablespoon olive oil
- ❖ ¼ cup red onion, sliced
- ❖ ½ cup green olives
- ❖ 2 oranges, peeled & sliced
- ❖ 3 celery stalks

Directions:
1. Put your oranges, olives, onion, and celery in a shallow bowl.
2. Blend oil, olive brine, and lemon juice, pour this over your salad.
3. Season with salt and pepper before serving.

Nutritional Information:
- ❖ 65 Calories
- ❖ 2g Protein
- ❖ 0.1g Fat

EYE-POPPING DESSERT

Thank you so much for your beautiful creation!! It was a real work of art!!

BOUNTY BARS

Preparation Time: 20 minutes
Cooking Time: 0 minutes
Servings: 12

Ingredients:
- ❖ 1 cup coconut cream
- ❖ 3 cups shredded unsweetened coconut
- ❖ 1/4 cup extra virgin coconut oil
- ❖ 1/2 teaspoon vanilla powder
- ❖ 1/4 cup powdered erythritol
- ❖ 1 1/2 oz. cocoa butter
- ❖ 5 oz. dark chocolate

Directions:
1. Heat the oven at 350 °F and toast the coconut in it for 5-6 minutes.
2. Remove from the oven once toasted and set aside to cool.
3. Take a medium-sized bowl and add coconut oil, coconut cream, vanilla, erythritol, and toasted coconut.
4. Mix the ingredients well to prepare a smooth mixture.
5. Make 12 bars of equal size with your hands from the prepared mixture and adjust in the tray lined with parchment paper.
6. Place the tray in the fridge within 1 hour. In the meantime, put the cocoa butter and dark chocolate in a glass bowl.
7. Simmer a cup of water in a saucepan over medium heat and place the bowl over it to melt the cocoa butter and the dark chocolate.
8. Remove from the heat once appropriately melted, mix well until blended, and set aside to cool.
9. Take the coconut bars and coat them with dark chocolate mixture one by one using a wooden stick.
10. Adjust on the tray lined with parchment paper and drizzle the remaining mixture over them.
11. Refrigerate for around one hour before you serve the delicious bounty bars.

Nutritional Information:
- ❖ Calories: 230
- ❖ Fat: 25 g
- ❖ Carbohydrates: 5 g
- ❖ Protein: 32 g

SHAKE CAKE

Preparation time: 15 minutes
Cooking time: 15 minutes
Servings: 1

Ingredients:
- ❖ 1 shake packet
- ❖ ¼ teaspoon baking powder
- ❖ 2 tablespoons egg beaters
- ❖ 2 tablespoons water
- ❖ 1 tablespoon reduced-fat cream cheese
- ❖ ½ packet Splenda

Directions:
1. Preheat the oven to 3500F.
2. Mix all ingredients in a bowl.
3. Pour in a muffin cup and bake for 15 minutes.
4. Allow cooling.

Nutritional Information:
- ❖ Calories: 271
- ❖ Protein: 8.7g
- ❖ Carbs: 19.4g
- ❖ Fat: 7.9g

AVOCADO KALE BOWL

Preparation Time: 10 minutes
Cooking Time: 0 minutes
Servings: 2

Ingredients:
- ❖ ½ avocado, sliced
- ❖ 1 cup kale leaves
- ❖ 1 banana, sliced
- ❖ ½ cup raspberries
- ❖ 1 cup almond milk
- ❖ 1 kiwi, sliced
- ❖ 2 drops stevia
- ❖ ½ cup ice
- ❖ 1 tsp chia seeds

Directions:
1. Place avocado, kale, stevia, banana, almond milk, and ice in a blender.
2. Process until smooth and creamy.
3. Transfer to a bowl. Serve and decorate the bowl by placing chia seeds, kiwi, and raspberries.

Nutritional Information:
- ❖ Calories: 230
- ❖ Fat: 1 g
- ❖ Carbohydrates: 12 g
- ❖ Protein: 15 g

BLUEBERRY LEMON CAKE

Preparation Time: 10 minutes
Cooking Time: 40 minutes
Servings: 4

Ingredients:
For the cake:
- ❖ 2/3 cup almond flour
- ❖ 5 eggs
- ❖ 1/3 cup almond milk, unsweetened
- ❖ ¼ cup erythritol
- ❖ 2 tsp. vanilla extract Juice of 2 lemons
- ❖ 1 tsp. lemon zest
- ❖ ½ tsp. baking soda
- ❖ Pinch of salt
- ❖ ½ cup fresh blueberries
- ❖ 2 tbsp. butter, melted

For the frosting:
- ❖ ½ cup heavy cream Juice of 1 lemon
- ❖ 1/8 cup erythritol

Directions:
1. Warm oven to 350F.
2. In a bowl, add the almond flour, eggs, and almond milk and mix well until smooth.
3. Add the erythritol, a pinch of salt, baking soda, lemon zest, lemon juice, and vanilla extract.
4. Mix and combine well.
5. Fold in the blueberries.
6. Use the butter to grease the pans.
7. Pour the batter into the greased pans, then put on a baking sheet for even baking.
8. Put in the oven to bake until cooked through and slightly brown on the top, about 35 to 40 minutes.
9. Let cool before removing from the pan.
10. Mix the erythritol, lemon juice, and heavy cream.
11. Mix well. Pour frosting on top.
12. Serve.

Nutritional Information:
- ❖ Calories:274
- ❖ Fat: 23 g
- ❖ Carbohydrates: 8 g

- ❖ Protein: 9 g

RICH CHOCOLATE MOUSSE

Preparation Time: 10 minutes
Cooking Time: 0 minutes
Servings: 3

Ingredients:
- ❖ ¼ cup low-fat coconut cream
- ❖ 2 cups fat-free Greek-style yogurt, strained
- ❖ 4 tsp. powered cocoa, no added sugar
- ❖ 2 tbsp. stevia/xylitol/bacon syrup
- ❖ 1 tsp. natural vanilla extract

Directions:
1. Mix all the fixings in a medium mixing bowl.
2. Put individual serving bowls or glasses and refrigerate.
3. Serve cold.

Nutritional Information:
- ❖ Calories: 269
- ❖ Fat: 3 g
- ❖ Carbohydrates: 20 g
- ❖ Protein: 43 g

RASPBERRY CHEESECAKE

Preparation Time: 10 minutes
Cooking Time: 25 minutes
Servings: 6

Ingredients:
- ❖ 2/3 cup coconut oil, melted
- ❖ ½ cup cream cheese
- ❖ 6 eggs
- ❖ 3 tbsp. granulated sweetener
- ❖ 1 tsp. vanilla extract
- ❖ ½ tsp. baking powder
- ❖ ¾ cup raspberries

Directions:
1. In a bowl, beat together the coconut oil and cream cheese until smooth.
2. Beat in eggs, then beat in the sweetener, vanilla, and baking powder until smooth.
3. Spoon the batter into the baking dish and smooth out the top.
4. Scatter the raspberries on top. Bake for 25 to 30 minutes or until the center is firm.
5. Cool, slice, and serve.

Nutritional Information:
- ❖ Calories: 176
- ❖ Fat: 18 g
- ❖ Carbohydrates: 3 g
- ❖ Protein: 6 g

APPLE COUSCOUS PUDDING

Preparation Time: 10 minutes
Cooking Time: 25 minutes
Servings: 4

Ingredients:
- ❖ ½ cup couscous
- ❖ 1 and ½ cups of milk
- ❖ ¼ cup apple, cored and chopped
- ❖ 3 tablespoons stevia
- ❖ ½ teaspoon rose water
- ❖ 1 tablespoon orange zest, grated

Directions:
1. Heat a pan with the milk over medium heat, add the couscous and the rest of the ingredients, whisk, simmer for 25 minutes, divide into bowls and serve.

Nutritional Information:
- ❖ Calories: 150
- ❖ Fat: 4.5g
- ❖ Carbs 7.5g
- ❖ Protein 4g

ALKALINE BLUEBERRY MUFFINS

Preparation Time: 5 Minutes
Cooking Time: 20 minutes
Servings: 3

Ingredients:
- ❖ 1 cup Coconut Milk
- ❖ 3/4 cup Spelt Flour
- ❖ 3/4 Teff Flour
- ❖ 1/2 cup Blueberries
- ❖ 1/3 cup Agave
- ❖ 1/4 cup Sea Moss Gel
- ❖ 1/2 tsp. Sea Salt
- ❖ Grapeseed Oil

Directions:
1. Adjust the temperature of the oven to 365 degrees.
2. Grease 6 regular-size muffin cups with muffin liners.
3. In a bowl, mix sea salt, sea moss, agave, coconut milk, and flour gel until they are properly blended.
4. You then crimp in blueberries.
5. Coat the muffin pan lightly with the grapeseed oil.
6. Pour in the muffin batter. Bake for at least 30 minutes until it turns golden brown.
7. Serve.

Nutritional Information:
- ❖ Calories: 160 kcal;
- ❖ Fat: 5g;
- ❖ Carbs: 25g;
- ❖ Proteins: 2g

VANILLA CAKE

Preparation Time: 5 minutes
Cooking time: 23 minutes
Servings: 12

Ingredients:
- ❖ 1 cup of condensed milk
- ❖ 1 cup evaporated milk
- ❖ 3 eggs
- ❖ 1 teaspoon vanilla extract

Cake:
- ❖ 2 cups of chocolate cake mix
- ❖ 2 eggs
- ❖ ¾ cup of nonfat milk Oil spray

Directions:
1. Blend condensed milk, evaporated milk, 3 eggs, and vanilla extract for 2 minutes.
2. Reserve this mix Cake
3. In the bowl, combine the cake mix, eggs, and milk with the help of the Balloon Whisk.
4. Reserve this preparation.
5. Preheat the pan at medium-high temperature for 3 minutes
6. Remove the pan from the stove for 1 minute and lightly spray the spray oil all over the surface - including the walls of the pan.
7. Add the cake mixture to the pan.
8. With the help of a spoon, pour the flan mixture evenly.
9. Put the pan back on the pot, reduce the temperature to low, cover with the valve closed, and cook for 23 minutes.
10. Let the pan rest for a few minutes.
11. Turn it carefully, so that the cake falls on a plate or flat surface.
12. Slice it and serve.

Nutritional Information:
- ❖ Calories: 84.62
- ❖ Carbohydrates: 1g
  Fat: 7.02g
- ❖ Protein: 3.71g
- ❖ Sugar: 0.64g
- ❖ Cholesterol: 97.43mg

HEALTHY COCONUT BLUEBERRY BALLS

Preparation Time: 10 minutes
Cooking time: 10 minutes
Servings: 12

Ingredients:
- ¼ cup flaked coconut
- ¼ cup blueberries
- ½ tsp vanilla
- ¼ cup honey
- ½ cup creamy almond butter
- ¼ tsp cinnamon
- 1 ½ tbsp chia seeds
- ¼ cup flaxseed meal
- 1 cup rolled oats, gluten-free

Directions:
1. In a large bowl, add oats, cinnamon, chia seeds, and flaxseed meal and mix well.
2. Add almond butter to a microwave-safe bowl and microwave for 30 seconds.
3. Stir until smooth.
4. Add vanilla and honey in melted almond butter and stir well.
5. Pour almond butter mixture over oat mixture and stir to combine.
6. Add coconut and blueberries and stir well.
7. Make small balls from the oat mixture and place them onto the baking tray
8. Serve and enjoy.

Nutritional Information:
- Calories 129,
- Fat: 7.4g,
- Carbohydrates: 14.1g,
- Sugar: 7g,
- Protein: 4 g,
- Cholesterol: 0 mg

CHOCOLATE MATCHA BALLS

Preparation Time: 10 minutes
Cooking time: 5 minutes
Servings: 15

Ingredients:
- ❖ 2 tbsp unsweetened cocoa powder
- ❖ 3 tbsp oats, gluten-free
- ❖ ½ cup pine nuts
- ❖ ½ cup almonds
- ❖ 1 cup dates, pitted
- ❖ 2 tbsp matcha powder

Directions:
1. Add oats, pine nuts, almonds, and dates into a food processor and process until well combined.
2. Place matcha powder in a small dish.
3. Make small balls from the mixture and coat with matcha powder.
4. Enjoy or store in the refrigerator until ready to eat.

Nutritional Information:
- ❖ Calories 88,
- ❖ Fat: 4.9g,
- ❖ Carbohydrates: 11.3g,
- ❖ Sugar: 7.8g,
- ❖ Protein: 1.9g,
- ❖ Cholesterol: 0mg

PISTACHIO AND FRUITS

Preparation Time: 5 minutes
Cooking time: 7 minutes
Servings: 12

Ingredients:
- ❖ ½ cup apricots, dried and chopped
- ❖ ¼ cup dried cranberries
- ❖ ½ tsp. cinnamon
- ❖ ¼ tsp. allspice
- ❖ ¼ tsp. ground nutmeg
- ❖ 1 ¼ cups unsalted pistachios, roasted
- ❖ 2 tsp. sugar

Directions:
1. Start by heating the oven to a temperature of around 345 degrees F.
2. Using a tray, place the pistachios, and bake for seven minutes.
3. Allow the pistachio to cool afterward.
4. Combine all ingredients in a container.
5. Once everything is combined well the food is ready to serve.

Nutritional Information:
- ❖ Calories: 377
- ❖ Carbohydrates: 24.5 g
- ❖ Fats: 5 g
- ❖ Proteins: 16 g

BUTTERED BANANA CHICKPEA

Preparation time: ten minutes
Cooking time: twelve minutes
Servings 8

Ingredients:
- ¼-tsp cinnamon
- ¼-tsp salt
- ⅓ -cup chocolate chips
- ⅓ -cup coconut sugar
- ½-cup creamy peanut butter
- 1-pc small banana, very ripe
- 1-tsp baking powder
- 2-Tbsps ground flaxseed
- 2-tsp vanilla extract fifteen-oz. chickpeas, washed and drained

Directions:
1. Preheat the oven to 350F.
2. Grease a baking pan with cooking spray.
3. Mix in all the ingredients apart from the chocolate chips in your blender.
4. Combine the batter for two minutes, or until turning into a smooth consistency.
5. Mix in the chocolate chips.
6. Ladle the batter to make cookies.
7. Put the cookies in the pan, and bake for about twelve minutes.

Nutritional Information:
- Calories: 372
- Fat: 12.4g
- Protein: 18.6g
- Sodium: 174mg
- Total Carbohydrates: 58.1g
- Fiber: 11.6g
- Net Carbohydrates: 46.5g

MY PICNIC DAYS

....
....
....
....
....
....
....
....
....
....
....
....
....
....
....
....
....
....
....
....
....
....
....
....
....

CPSIA information can be obtained
at www.ICGtesting.com
Printed in the USA
LVHW101037270521
688665LV00017B/1085

9 781802 931488